Modern Critical Interpretations
Beowulf

Modern Critical Interpretations

These and other titles in preparation

Modern Critical Interpretations

Beowulf

Edited and with an introduction by
Harold Bloom
Sterling Professor of the Humanities
Yale University

Chelsea House Publishers
NEW YORK ◊ PHILADELPHIA

© 1987 by Chelsea House Publishers, a division
of Main Line Book Co.

Introduction © 1987 by Harold Bloom

Printed and bound in the United States of America

10 9 8 7 6 5 4 3 2

∞ The paper used in this publication meets the minimum
requirements of the American National Standard for Permanence
of Paper for Printed Library Materials, Z39.48–1984.

Library of Congress Cataloging-in-Publication Data
Beowulf.
   (Modern critical interpretations)
   Bibliography: p.
   Includes index.
   1. Beowulf. 2. Epic poetry, English (Old)—History and
criticism. I. Bloom, Harold. II. Series.
PR1585.B38 1987   829'.3   87–8093
ISBN 0–87754–904–4 (alk. paper)

Contents

Editor's Note

This book gathers together a representative selection of the best modern criticism of the Old English epic *Beowulf*. The critical essays are reprinted here in the chronological order of their original publication. I am grateful to Marena Fisher for her aid in editing this volume.

My introduction follows E. Talbot Donaldson in his contention that *Beowulf* is a barely Christian poem, and takes mild exception to the subtle and advanced reading by Fred C. Robinson, who argues that the epic juxtaposes Christian and pagan perspectives through an appositional style. J. R. R. Tolkien, seer of hobbits, begins the chronological sequence with his famous essay defending *Beowulf*'s splendid monsters against some of the poem's less splendid critics.

An overview of the cosmos of *Beowulf* by T. A. Shippey is followed by Roberta Frank's illumination of the rather difficult sense of history displayed by the *Beowulf* poet and by Raymond P. Tripp, Jr.'s exegesis of the function of digressions in the poem.

The summit of *Beowulf* criticism to date is represented here by Fred C. Robinson on the poem's rhetoric of appositions, to which I have stated some admiring objections in my introduction. This book concludes with Ian Duncan's previously unpublished account of *Beowulf*'s own elegiac relation to Germanic origins, which he sees as fading away beautifully as the poem progresses.

Introduction

Whether any particular poem can be termed "Christian" or even "religious" is a much more problematical question than we tend to recognize. *Beowulf* is generally judged to be a Christian poem on a Germanic hero. I myself would deny that even *Paradise Lost* is a Christian poem, because John Milton was a Protestant sect of one, and his epic reflects his highly individual spiritual stance. More crucially, the distinction between a sacred and a secular poem never seems to me a *poetic* distinction. You can regard all strong poetry as being religious, or all strong poetry as being secular, but to judge one authentic poem as being more religious or more secular than another seems to me a societal or political matter rather than an aesthetic finding.

Why then care whether or not *Beowulf* is a Christian, as well as being a heroic poem? The answer is partly historical, partly imaginative or poetic. During the first half of the fifth century the Angles, Saxons, and Jutes overran Roman Britain. By the end of the seventh century these Germans, and the Celts they ruled, mostly had been converted to Christianity. *Beowulf* is assigned by some scholars to the first half of the eighth century, and its nameless author undoubtedly was a Christian, at least nominally. But if *Beowulf* is to be considered a Christian poem, we must ask, Can there be Christianity without the figure of Jesus Christ, and without the presence of the New Testament? Every biblical allusion in *Beowulf,* all scholars agree, is to what Christians call the Old Testament. E. Talbot Donaldson, distinguished scholar-critic of medieval English literature, expresses this oddity with his usual laconic good sense:

> Yet there is no reference to the New Testament—to Christ and His Sacrifice which are the real bases of Christianity in any intelligible sense of the term. Furthermore, readers may well feel that the poem achieves rather little of its emotional

1

power through invocation of Christian values or of values that are consonant with Christian doctrine as we know it. . . .

. . . One must, indeed, draw the conclusion from the poem itself that while Christian is a correct term for the religion of the poet and of his audience, it was a Christianity that had not yet by any means succeeded in obliterating an older pagan tradition, which still called forth powerful responses from men's hearts, despite the fact that many aspects of this tradition must be abhorrent to a sophisticated Christian.

I first read *Beowulf* thirty-five years ago, as a graduate student, and have just reread it, cheerfully using Donaldson's splendid prose translation to eke out my faded command of the text. Certainly Donaldson describes what I have read: a heroic poem celebrating the same values that Tacitus discerned in the Germans of his day. Courage is the prime virtue exalted in *Beowulf*. No one reading the poem would find Beowulf to be a particularly Christian hero. His glory has little to do with worship, unless it be justified self-worship, and he fights primarily for glory, to increase his fame, to show that he occupies the foremost place among all Germanic heroes. It is true that Grendel and his even more monstrous mother are portrayed for us as descendants of Cain, but neither they nor the fatal dragon at the poem's end can be said to fight against Christ, or the things that are Christ's. When Beowulf goes forth to battle, he is in quest of reputation and treasure, but not of Christ or God or the truth.

The subtlest defense of a Christian reading of *Beowulf* is by Fred C. Robinson, who finds in the poem an appositive style that balances Dark Age heroism and Christian regret, and that enables the poet to "communicate his Christian vision of pagan heroic life." The dominant tone of *Beowulf,* according to Robinson, is one of "combined admiration and regret" for heroic paganism, as it were. The Christian present confronts the Germanic past, admires its heroism, and supposedly regrets its paganism. In much the most sophisticated critical reading yet afforded the poem, Robinson sets out to correct the view of Tolkien, who somehow could give us Hrothgar as Christian surrounded by pagan companions:

Because Hrothgar advises Beowulf against overweening pride, avarice, and irascible violence, some scholars have wanted to see this as a Christian homily on the Seven Deadly Sins, and many parallels in Scripture and commentary have been adduced. But there is nothing in the speech that is not equally accordant with Germanic pre-Christian piety.

For Robinson, the entire poem manifests a double perspective of a remarkable kind:

> Reading *Beowulf* is, in a way, like reading the centos of Proba, Luxorius and Pomponius, who composed entire poems on Christian subjects by rearranging the verses of Virgil, Horace, and Ovid in order to make them convey Christian meanings. Students of these curious works hold two contexts in mind at the same time, for their pleasure is in following the Christian level of the narrative while remaining aware of the source of the poetic language. Just as in reading the centos we think simultaneously of Aeneas and Christ, so in reading *Beowulf* we should hear distant echoes of Thunor and Woden when the men of old appeal to their "mihtig dryhten" and "fæder al-walda." We know to whom these words refer in the Christian present, but we also know that they once referred to other, darker beings.

A polysemous theological diction thus dominates *Beowulf,* just as it does *Paradise Lost,* if Robinson is wholly correct. Holding Christian and pagan terms in patterns of apposition, the *Beowulf* poet is able to imply Christian values without repudiating ancestral virtues, and yet, in Robinson's judgment, the poem ends upon a kind of modified repudiation, with the statement that Beowulf was *lofgeornost,* translated by Donaldson as "most eager for fame." To say with your last word that the hero, above all men, desired to be praised, wanted a glory bestowed by his fellows, is to insinuate that the hero is wanting, by Christian standards. To maintain his case, Robinson is compelled to this reading, which seems to me to possess a fine desperation:

> The people of Christian England can never reenter the severe, benighted world of the men of old, nor would they. All the poetry of *Beowulf* can do is bring the two together in a brief, loving, and faintly disquieting apposition.

But here is the conclusion of *Beowulf,* in Donaldson's translation:

> Then the people of the Weather-Geats built a mound on the promontory, one that was high and broad, wide-seen by sea-farers, and in ten days completed a monument for the bold in battle, surrounded the remains of the fire with a wall, the most splendid that men most skilled might devise. In the bar-

row they placed rings and jewels, all such ornaments as troubled men had earlier taken from the hoard. They let the earth hold the wealth of earls, gold in the ground, where now it still dwells, as useless to men as it was before. Then the brave in battle rode round the mound, children of nobles, twelve in all, would bewail their sorrow and mourn their king, recite dirges and speak of the man. They praised his great deeds and his acts of courage, judged well of his prowess. So it is fitting that man honor his liege lord with words, love him in heart when he must be led forth from the body. Thus the people of the Geats, his hearth-companions, lamented the death of their lord. They said that he was of world-kings the mildest of men and the gentlest, kindest to his people, and most eager for fame.

Does this indeed end with a disquieting apposition? Do we feel that the mildness, gentleness, and kindness of Beowulf (to *his* people, not to monsters, enemies, traitors, or whatever) is in apposition to his lust for renown? Heroic poetry can do little with the virtues of the New Testament Christ, though considerably more with certain epic qualities of the Old Testament. The *Beowulf* poet may have felt no personal nostalgia for the beliefs of his Germanic ancestors, but after all he had chosen to write a heroic poem rather than a work on the finding of the True Cross. Is a poem Christian only because it undoubtedly was written by a Christian? There is nothing about God's grace in *Beowulf,* though something about God's glory as a creator. And there is much tribute to Fate, hardly a Christian category, and rarely is Fate set in apposition with the will of God, as Robinson's pattern might lead us to expect.

Rereading *Beowulf* gives one a fierce and somber sense of heroic loss, in a grim world, not wholly unlike the cosmos of Virgil's *Aeneid*. In spirit, the poem does seem to me more Virgilian than Christian. Though addressed to a Christian audience, it seems not to be addressed to them *as* Christians but as descendants of heroic warriors. Beowulf does not die so as to advance the truth but so as to maintain his own glory, the fame of a man who could slay a monster with only his own bare hands to do the heroic work. The bareness of those unfaltering hands counts for much more than does the monster's descent from the wicked line of the accursed Cain.

*B*eowulf: The Monsters and the Critics

J. R. R. Tolkien

In 1864 the Reverend Oswald Cockayne wrote of the Reverend Doctor Joseph Bosworth, Rawlinsonian Professor of Anglo-Saxon: "I have tried to lend to others the conviction I have long entertained that Dr Bosworth is not a man so diligent in his special walk as duly to read the books . . . which have been printed in our old English, or so-called Anglosaxon tongue. He may do very well for a professor." These words were inspired by dissatisfaction with Bosworth's dictionary, and were doubtless unfair. If Bosworth were still alive, a modern Cockayne would probably accuse him of not reading the "literature" of his subject, the books written about the books in the so-called Anglo-Saxon tongue. The original books are nearly buried.

Of none is this so true as of *The Beowulf,* as it used to be called. I have, of course, read *The Beowulf,* as have most (but not all) of those who have criticized it. But I fear that, unworthy successor and beneficiary of Joseph Bosworth, I have not been a man so diligent in my special walk as duly to read all that has been printed on, or touching on, this poem. But I have read enough, I think, to venture the opinion that *Beowulfiana* is, while rich in many departments, specially poor in one. It is poor in criticism, criticism that is directed to the understanding of a poem as a poem. It has been said of *Beowulf* itself that its weakness lies in placing the unimportant things at the centre and the important on the outer edges. This is one of the opinions that I wish specially to consider.

From *The Monsters and the Critics and Other Essays,* edited by Christopher Tolkien. © 1983 by Frank Richard Williamson and Christopher Reuel Tolkien as Executors of the Estate of J. R. R. Tolkien. George Allen & Unwin (Publishers) Ltd., 1983. Translations supplied by the editor.

I think it profoundly untrue of the poem, but strikingly true of the literature about it. *Beowulf* has been used as a quarry of fact and fancy far more assiduously than it has been studied as a work of art.

It is of *Beowulf,* then, as a poem that I wish to speak; and though it may seem presumption that I should try with *swich a lewed mannes wit to pace the wisdom of an heep of lerned men,* in this department there is at least more chance for the *lewed man.* But there is so much that might still be said even under these limitations that I shall confine myself mainly to the *monsters*—Grendel and the Dragon, as they appear in what seems to me the best and most authoritative general criticism in English—and to certain considerations of the structure and conduct of the poem that arise from this theme.

There is an historical explanation of the state of *Beowulfiana* that I have referred to. And that explanation is important, if one would venture to criticize the critics. A sketch of the history of the subject is required. But I will here only attempt, for brevity's sake, to present my view of it allegorically. As it set out upon its adventures among the modern scholars, *Beowulf* was christened by Wanley Poesis—*Poeseos Anglo-Saxonicæ egregium exemplum.* But the fairy godmother later invited to superintend its fortunes was Historia. And she brought with her Philologia, Mythologia, Archaeologia, and Laographia. Excellent ladies. But where was the child's name-sake? Poesis was usually forgotten; occasionally admitted by a side-door; sometimes dismissed upon the door-step. "*The Beowulf,*" they said, "is hardly an affair of yours, and not in any case a protégé that you could be proud of. It is an historical document. Only as such does it interest the superior culture of today." And it is as an historical document that it has mainly been examined and dissected. Though ideas as to the nature and quality of the history and information embedded in it have changed much since Thorkelin called it *De Danorum Rebus Gestis,* this has remained steadily true. In still recent pronouncements this view is explicit. In 1925 Professor Archibald Strong translated *Beowulf* into verse; but in 1921 he had declared: "*Beowulf* is the picture of a whole civilization, of the Germania which Tacitus describes. The main interest which the poem has for us is thus not a purely literary interest. *Beowulf* is an important historical document."

I make this preliminary point, because it seems to me that the air has been clouded not only for Strong, but for other more authoritative critics, by the dust of the quarrying researchers. It may well be asked: why should we approach this, or indeed any other poem, mainly as an historical document? Such an attitude is defensible: firstly, if one is not concerned with poetry at all, but seeking information wherever it may be found; secondly, if the so-called poem contains in fact no poetry. I am not concerned with the first case. The historian's search is, of course, perfectly legitimate, even if it does not assist criticism in general at all (for that is not its object), so long as it is not mistaken for criticism. To Professor Birger Nerman as an historian of Swedish origins *Beowulf* is doubtless an important document, but he is not writing a history of English poetry. Of the second case it may be said that to rate a poem, a thing at the least in metrical form, as mainly of historical interest should *in a literary survey* be equivalent to saying that it has no literary merits, and little more need in such a survey then be said about it. But such a judgement on *Beowulf* is false. So far from being a poem so poor that only its accidental historical interest can still recommend it, *Beowulf* is in fact so interesting as poetry, in places poetry so powerful, that this quite overshadows the historical content, and is largely independent even of the most important facts (such as the date and identity of Hygelac) that research has discovered. It is indeed a curious fact that it is one of the peculiar poetic virtues of *Beowulf* that has contributed to its own critical misfortunes. The illusion of historical truth and perspective, that has made *Beowulf* seem such an attractive quarry, is largely a product of art. The author has used an instinctive historical sense—a part indeed of the ancient English temper (and not unconnected with its reputed melancholy), of which *Beowulf* is a supreme expression; but he has used it with a poetical and not an historical object. The lovers of poetry can safely study the art, but the seekers after history must beware lest the glamour of Poesis overcome them.

Nearly all the censure, and most of the praise, that has been bestowed on *The Beowulf* has been due either to the belief that it was something that it was *not*—for example, primitive, pagan, Teutonic, an allegory (political or mythical), or most often, an epic; or to disappointment at the discovery that it was itself and not something that the scholar would have liked better—for example, a heathen heroic lay, a history of Sweden, a manual of Germanic antiquities, or a Nordic *Summa Theologica*.

I would express the whole industry in yet another allegory. A man inherited a field in which was an accumulation of old stone, part of an older hall. Of the old stone some had already been used in building the house in which he actually lived, not far from the old house of his fathers. Of the rest he took some and built a tower. But his friends coming perceived at once (without troubling to climb the steps) that these stones had formerly belonged to a more ancient building. So they pushed the tower over, with no little labour, in order to look for hidden carvings and inscriptions, or to discover whence the man's distant forefathers had obtained their building material. Some suspecting a deposit of coal under the soil began to dig for it, and forgot even the stones. They all said: "This tower is most interesting." But they also said (after pushing it over): "What a muddle it is in!" And even the man's own descendants, who might have been expected to consider what he had been about, were heard to murmur: "He is such an odd fellow! Imagine his using these old stones just to build a nonsensical tower! Why did not he restore the old house? He had no sense of proportion." But from the top of that tower the man had been able to look out upon the sea.

I hope I shall show that that allegory is just—even when we consider the more recent and more perceptive critics (whose concern is in intention with literature). To reach these we must pass in rapid flight over the heads of many decades of critics. As we do so a conflicting babel mounts up to us, which I can report as something after this fashion. "*Beowulf* is a half-baked native epic the development of which was killed by Latin learning; it was inspired by emulation of Virgil, and is a product of the education that came in with Christianity; it is feeble and incompetent as a narrative; the rules of narrative are cleverly observed in the manner of the learned epic; it is the confused product of a committee of muddle-headed and probably beer-bemused Anglo-Saxons (this is a Gallic voice); it is a string of pagan lays edited by monks; it is the work of a learned but inaccurate Christian antiquarian; it is a work of genius, rare and surprising in the period, though the genius seems to have been shown principally in doing something much better left undone (this is a very recent voice); it is a wild folk-tale (general chorus); it is a poem of an aristocratic and courtly tradition (same voices); it is a hotch-potch; it is a sociological, anthropological, archaeological document; it is a mythical allegory (very old voices these and generally shouted down, but not so far out as some of the newer cries); it is rude and rough; it is a masterpiece of metrical art; it has no shape at all; it is singularly weak in construction; it is a clever allegory of contemporary politics (old John Earle with some slight support from Mr Girvan, only they look to different periods); its architecture is solid; it is thin and cheap (a solemn voice); it is undeniably weighty (the same voice); it is a national epic; it is a translation from the Danish; it was imported by Frisian traders; it is a burden to English syllabuses; and (final universal chorus of all voices) it is worth studying."

It is not surprising that it should now be felt that a view, a decision, a conviction are imperatively needed. But it is plainly only in the consideration of *Beowulf* as a poem, with an inherent poetic significance, that any view or conviction can be reached or steadily held. For it is of their nature that the jabberwocks of historical and antiquarian research burble in the tulgy wood of conjecture, flitting from one tum-tum tree to another. Noble animals, whose burbling is on occasion good to hear; but though their eyes of flame may sometimes prove searchlights, their range is short.

None the less, paths of a sort have been opened in the wood. Slowly with the rolling years the obvious (so often the last revelation of analytic study) has been discovered: that we have to deal with a poem by an Englishman using afresh ancient and largely traditional material. At last then, after inquiring so long whence this material came, and what its original or aboriginal nature was (questions that cannot ever be decisively answered), we might also now again inquire what the poet did with it. If we ask that question, then there is still, perhaps, something lacking even in the major critics, the learned and revered masters from whom we humbly derive.

The chief points with which I feel dissatisfied I will now approach by way of W. P. Ker, whose name and memory I honour. He would deserve reverence, of course, even if he still lived and had not "ellor gehworfen on Frean wære [gone elsewhere into the Lord's protection]" upon a high mountain in the heart of that Europe which he loved: a great scholar, as illuminating himself as a critic, as he was often biting as a critic of the critics. None the less I cannot help feeling that in approaching *Beowulf* he was hampered by the almost inevitable weakness of his greatness: stories and plots must sometimes have seemed triter to him, the much-read, than they did to the old poets and their audiences. The dwarf on the spot sometimes sees things missed by the travelling giant ranging many countries. In considering a period when literature was narrower in range and men possessed a less diversified stock of ideas and themes, one must seek to recapture and esteem the deep pondering and profound feeling that they gave to such as they possessed.

In any case Ker has been potent. For his criticism is masterly, expressed always in words both pungent and weighty, and not least so when it is (as I occasionally venture to think) itself open to criticism. His words and judgements are often quoted, or reappear in various modifications, digested, their source probably sometimes forgotten. It is impossible to avoid quotation of the well-known passage in his *Dark Ages*:

A reasonable view of the merit of *Beowulf* is not impossible, though rash enthusiasm may have made too much of it, while a correct and sober taste may have too contemptuously refused to attend to Grendel or the Fire-drake. The fault of *Beowulf* is that there is nothing much in the story. The hero is occupied in killing monsters, like Hercules or Theseus. But there are other things in the lives of Hercules and Theseus besides the killing of the Hydra or of Procrustes. Beowulf has nothing else to do, when he has killed Grendel and Grendel's mother in Denmark: he goes home to his own Gautland, until at last the rolling years bring the Fire-drake and his last adventure. It is too simple. Yet the three chief episodes are well wrought and well diversified; they are not repetitions, exactly; there is a change of temper between the wrestling with Grendel in the night at Heorot and the descent under water to encounter Grendel's mother; while the sentiment of the Dragon is different again. But the great beauty, the real value, of *Beowulf* is in its dignity of style. In construction it is curiously weak, in a sense preposterous; for while the main story is simplicity itself, the merest commonplace of heroic legend, all about it, in the historic allusions, there are revelations of a whole world of tragedy, plots different in import from that of *Beowulf,* more like the tragic themes of Iceland. Yet with this radical defect, a disproportion that puts the irrelevances in the centre and the serious things on the outer edges, the poem of *Beowulf* is undeniably weighty. The thing itself is cheap; the moral and the spirit of it can only be matched among the noblest authors.

This passage was written more than thirty years ago, but has hardly been surpassed. It remains, in this country at any rate, a potent influence. Yet its primary effect is to state a paradox which one feels has always strained the belief, even of those who accepted it, and has given to *Beowulf* the character of an "enigmatic poem." The chief virtue of the passage (not the one for which it is usually esteemed) is that it does accord some attention to the monsters, despite correct and sober taste. But the contrast made between the radical defect of theme and structure, and at the same time the dignity, loftiness in converse, and well-wrought finish, has become a commonplace even of the best criticism, a paradox the strangeness of which has almost been forgotten in the process of swallowing it upon authority. We may compare Professor Chambers in his *Widsith,* where he is studying the story of Ingeld, son of Froda, and his feud with the great Scylding house of Denmark, a story introduced in *Beowulf* merely as an allusion.

> Nothing [Chambers says] could better show the disproportion of *Beowulf* which "puts the irrelevances in the centre and the serious things on the outer edges," than this passing allusion to the story of Ingeld. For in this conflict between plighted troth and the duty of revenge we have a situation which the old heroic poets loved, and would not have sold for a wilderness of dragons.

I pass over the fact that the allusion has a dramatic purpose in *Beowulf* that is a sufficient defence both of its presence and of its manner. The author of *Beowulf* cannot be held responsible for the fact that we now have only his poem and not others dealing primarily with Ingeld. He was not selling one thing for another, but giving something new. But let us return to the dragon. "A wilderness of dragons." There is a sting in this Shylockian plural, the sharper for coming from a critic, who deserves the title of the poet's best friend. It is in the tradition of the Book of St Albans, from which the poet might retort upon his critics: "Yea, a desserte of lapwyngs, a shrewednes of apes, a raffull of knaues, and a gagle of gees."

As for the poem, one dragon, however hot, does not make a summer, or a host; and a man might well exchange for one good dragon what he would not sell for a wilderness. And dragons, real dragons, essential both to the machinery and the ideas of a poem or tale, are actually rare. In Northern literature there are only *two* that are significant. If we omit from consideration the vast and vague Encircler of the World, Migarsormr, the doom of the great gods and no matter for heroes, we have but the dragon of the Völsungs, Fáfnir, and Beowulf's bane. It is true that both of these are in *Beowulf*, one in the main story, and the other spoken of by a minstrel praising Beowulf himself. But this is not a wilderness of dragons. Indeed the allusion to the more renowned worm killed by the Wælsing is sufficient indication that the poet selected a dragon of well-founded purpose (or saw its significance in the plot as it had reached him), even as he was careful to compare his hero, Beowulf son of Ecgtheow, to the prince of the heroes of the North, the dragon-slaying Wælsing. He esteemed dragons, as rare as they are dire, as some do still. He liked them—as a poet, not as a sober zoologist; and he had good reason.

But we meet this kind of criticism again. In Chambers's *Beowulf and the Heroic Age*—the most significant single essay on the poem that I know—it is still present. The riddle is still unsolved. The folk-tale motive stands still like the spectre of old research, dead but unquiet in its grave. We are told again that the main story of *Beowulf* is a *wild folk-tale*. Quite true, of course. It is true of the main story of *King Lear*, unless in that case you would prefer to substitute *silly* for *wild*. But more: we are told that the same sort of stuff is found in Homer, yet there it is kept in its proper place. "The folk-tale is a good servant," Chambers says, and does not perhaps realize the importance of the admission, made to save the face of Homer and Virgil; for he continues: "but a bad master: it has been allowed in *Beowulf* to usurp the place of honour, and to drive into episodes and digressions the things which should be the main stuff of a well-conducted epic." It is not clear to me why good *conduct* must depend on the main *stuff*. But I will for the moment remark only that, if it is so, *Beowulf* is evidently not a well-conducted epic. It may turn out to be no epic at all. But the puzzle still continues. In the most recent discourse upon this theme it still appears, toned down almost to a melancholy question-mark, as if this paradox had at last begun to afflict with weariness the thought that endeavours to support it. In the final peroration of his notable lecture on *Folk-tale and History in Beowulf*, given last year, Mr Girvan said:

> Confessedly there is matter for wonder and scope for doubt, but we might be able to answer with complete satisfaction some of the questionings which rise in men's minds over the poet's presentment of his hero, if we could also answer with certainty the question why he chose just this subject, when to our modern judgment there were at hand so many greater, charged with the splendour and tragedy of humanity, and in all respects worthier of a genius as astonishing as it was rare in Anglo-Saxon England.

There is something irritatingly odd about all this. One even dares to wonder if something has not gone wrong with "our modern judgement," supposing that it is justly represented. Higher praise than is found in the learned critics, whose scholarship enables them to appreciate these things, could hardly be given to the detail, the tone, the style, and indeed to the total effect of *Beowulf*. Yet this poetic talent, we are to understand, has all been squandered on an unprofitable theme: as if Milton had recounted the story of Jack and the Beanstalk in noble verse. Even if Milton had done this (and he might have done worse), we should perhaps pause to consider whether his poetic handling had not had some effect upon the trivial theme; what alchemy had been performed upon the base metal; whether indeed it remained base or trivial when he had finished with it. The high tone, the sense of dignity, alone is evidence in *Beowulf* of the presence of a mind lofty and thoughtful. It is, one would have said, improbable that such a man would write more than three thousand lines (wrought to a high finish) on matter that is really not worth serious attention; that remains thin and cheap when he has finished with it. Or that he should in the selection of his material, in the choice of what to put forward, what to keep subordinate "upon the outer edges," have shown a puerile simplicity much below the level of the characters he himself draws in his own poem. Any theory that will at least allow us to believe that what he did was of design, and that for that design there is a defence that may still have force, would seem more probable.

It has been too little observed that all the machinery of "dignity" is to be found elsewhere. Cynewulf, or the author of *Andreas,* or of *Guthlac* (most notably), have a command of dignified verse. In them there is well-wrought language, weighty words, lofty sentiment, precisely that which we are told is the real beauty of *Beowulf.* Yet it cannot, I think, be disputed, that *Beowulf* is more beautiful, that each line there is more significant (even when, as sometimes happens, it is the same line) than in the other long Old English poems. Where then resides the special virtue of *Beowulf,* if the common element (which belongs largely to the language itself, and to a literary tradition) is deducted? It resides, one might guess, in the theme, and the spirit this has infused into the whole. For, in fact, if there were a real discrepancy between theme and style, that style would not be felt as beautiful but as incongruous or false. And that incongruity is present in some measure in all the long Old English poems, save one—*Beowulf.* The paradoxical contrast that has been drawn between matter and manner in *Beowulf* has thus an inherent *literary* improbability.

Why then have the great critics thought otherwise? I must pass rather hastily over the answers to this question. The reasons are various, I think, and would take long to examine. I believe that one reason is that the shadow of research has lain upon criticism. The habit, for instance, of pondering a summarized plot of *Beowulf,* denuded of all that gives it particular force or individual life, has encouraged the notion that its main story is wild, or trivial, or typical, *even after treatment.* Yet all stories, great and small, are one or more of these three things in such nakedness. The comparison of skeleton "plots" is simply not a critical literary process at all. It has been favoured by research in comparative folk-lore, the objects of which are primarily historical or scientific. Another reason is, I think, that the allusions have attracted curiosity (antiquarian rather than critical) to their elucidation; and this needs so much study and research that attention has been diverted from the poem as a whole, and from the function of the allusions, as shaped and placed, in the poetic economy of *Beowulf* as it is. Yet actually the appreciation of this function is largely independent of such investigations.

But there is also, I suppose, a real question of taste involved: a judgement that the heroic or tragic story on a strictly human plane is by nature superior. Doom is held less literary than ἁμαρτία [hamartia]. The proposition seems to have been passed as self-evident. I dissent, even at the risk of being held incorrect or not sober. But I will not here enter into debate, nor attempt at length a defence of the mythical mode of imagination, and the disentanglement of the confusion between myth and folk-tale into which these judgements appear to have fallen. The myth has other forms than the (now discredited) mythical allegory of nature: the sun, the seasons, the sea, and such things. The term "folk-tale" is misleading; its very tone of depreciation begs the question. Folk-tales in being, as told—for the "typical folk-tale," of course, is merely an abstract conception of research nowhere existing—do often contain elements that are thin and cheap, with little even potential virtue; but they also contain much that is far more powerful, and that cannot be sharply separated from myth, being derived from it, or capable in poetic hands of turning into it: that is of becoming largely significant—as a whole, accepted unanalysed. The significance of a myth is not easily to be pinned on paper by analytical reasoning. It is at its best when it is presented by a poet who feels rather than makes explicit what his theme portends; who presents it incarnate in the world of history and geography, as our poet has done. Its defender is thus at a disadvantage: unless he is careful, and speaks in parables, he will kill what he is studying by vivisection, and he will be left with a formal or mechanical allegory, and, what is more, probably with one that will not work. For myth is alive at once and in all its parts, and dies before it can be dissected. It is possible, I think, to be moved by the power of myth and yet to misunderstand the sensation, to ascribe it wholly to something else that is also present: to metrical art, style, or verbal skill. Correct and sober taste may refuse to admit that there can be an interest for *us*—the proud *we* that includes all intelligent living people—in ogres and dragons; we then perceive its puzzlement in face of the odd fact that it has derived great pleasure from a poem that is actually about these unfashionable creatures. Even though it attributes "genius," as does Mr Girvan, to the author, it cannot admit that the monsters are anything but a sad mistake.

It does not seem plain that ancient taste supports the modern as much as it has been represented to do. I have the author of *Beowulf,* at any rate, on my side: a greater man than most of us. And I cannot myself perceive a period in the North when one kind alone was esteemed: there was room for myth and heroic legend, and for blends of these. As for the dragon: as far as we know anything about these old poets, we know this: the prince of the heroes of the North, supremely memorable—"hans nafn mun uppi meðan veröldin stendr [his name will be remembered as long as the world stands]"—was a dragon-slayer. And his most renowned deed, from which in Norse he derived his title Fáfnisbani, was the slaying of the prince of legendary worms. Although there is plainly considerable difference between the later Norse and the ancient English form of the story alluded to in *Beowulf,* already there it had these two primary features: the dragon, and the slaying of him as the chief deed of the greatest of heroes—"he wæs wreccena wide mærost [he was of adventurers famous far and wide]." A dragon is no idle fancy. Whatever may be his origins, in fact or invention, the dragon in legend is a potent creation of men's imagination, richer in significance than his barrow is in gold. Even to-day (despite the critics) you may find men not ignorant of tragic legend and history, who have heard of heroes and indeed seen them, who yet have been caught by the fascination of the worm. More than one poem in recent years (since *Beowulf* escaped somewhat from the dominion of the students of origins to the students of poetry) has been inspired by the dragon of *Beowulf,* but none that I know of by Ingeld son of Froda. Indeed, I do not think Chambers very happy in his particular choice. He gives battle on dubious ground. In so far as we can now grasp its detail and atmosphere the story of Ingeld the thrice faithless and easily persuaded is chiefly interesting as an episode in a larger theme, as part of a tradition that had acquired legendary, and so dramatically personalized, form concerning moving events in history: the arising of Denmark, and wars in the islands of the North. In itself it is not a supremely potent story. But, of course, as with all tales of any sort, its literary power must have depended mainly upon how it was handled. A poet may have made a great thing of it. Upon this chance must be founded the popularity of Ingeld's legend in England, for which there is some evidence. There is no inherent magical virtue about heroic-tragic stories as such, and apart from the merits of individual treatments. The same heroic plot can yield good and bad poems, and good and bad sagas. The recipe for the central situations of such stories, studied in the abstract, is after all as "simple" and as "typical" as that of folk-tales. There are in any case many heroes but very few good dragons.

Beowulf's dragon, if one wishes really to criticize, is not to be blamed for being a dragon, but rather for not being dragon enough, plain pure fairy-story dragon. There are in the poem some vivid touches of the right kind—as "þa se wyrm onwoc, wroht wæs geniwad; stonc æfter stane [when the worm awoke, strife was renewed; he moved quickly over the stone]" (l. 2285)—in which this dragon is real worm, with a bestial life and thought of his own, but the conception, none the less, approaches *draconitas* rather than *draco*: a personification of malice, greed, destruction (the evil side of heroic life), and of the undiscriminating cruelty of fortune that distinguishes not good or bad (the evil aspect of all life). But for *Beowulf,* the poem, that is as it should be. In this poem the balance is nice, but it is preserved. The large symbolism is near the surface, but it does not break through, nor become allegory. Something more signifi-cant than a standard hero, a man faced with a foe more evil than any human enemy of house or realm, is before us, and yet incarnate in time, walking in heroic history, and treading the named lands of the North. And this, we are told, is the radical defect of *Beowulf,* that its author, coming in a time rich in the legends of heroic men, has used them afresh in an original fashion, giving us not just one more, but something akin yet different: a measure and interpretation of them all.

We do not deny the worth of the hero by accepting Grendel and the dragon. Let us by all means esteem the old heroes: men caught in the chains of circumstance or of their own character, torn between duties equally sacred, dying with their backs to the wall. But *Beowulf,* I fancy, plays a larger part than is recognized in helping us to esteem them. Heroic lays may have dealt in their own way—we have little enough to judge by—a way more brief and vigorous, perhaps, though perhaps also more harsh and noisy (and less thoughtful), with the actions of heroes caught in circumstances that conformed more or less to the varied but funda-mentally simple recipe for an heroic situation. In these (if we had them) we could see the exaltation of undefeated will, which receives doctrinal expression in the words of Byrhtwold at the battle of Maldon. But though with sympathy and patience we might gather, from a line here or a tone there, the background of imagination which gives to this indomitability, this paradox of defeat inevitable yet unacknowledged, its full significance, it is in *Beowulf* that a poet has devoted a whole poem to the theme, and has drawn the struggle in different proportions, so that we may see man at war with the hostile world, and his inevitable overthrow in Time. The particular is on the outer edge, the essential in the centre.

Of course, I do not assert that the poet, if questioned, would have replied in the Anglo-Saxon equivalents of these terms. Had the matter been so explicit to him, his poem would certainly have been the worse. None the less we may still, against his great scene, hung with tapestries woven of ancient tales of ruin, see the *hæleð* walk. When we have read his poem, as a poem, rather than as a collection of episodes, we perceive that he who wrote *hæleð under heofenum* may have meant in dictionary terms "heroes under heaven," or "mighty men upon earth," but he and his hearers were thinking of the *eormengrund*, the great earth, ringed with *garsecg*, the shoreless sea, beneath the sky's inaccessible roof; whereon, as in a little circle of light about their halls, men with courage as their stay went forward to that battle with the hostile world and the offspring of the dark which ends for all, even the kings and champions, in defeat. That even this "geography," once held as a material fact, could now be classed as a mere folk-tale affects its value very little. It transcends astronomy. Not that astronomy has done anything to make the island seem more secure or the outer seas less formidable.

Beowulf is not, then, the hero of an heroic lay, precisely. He has no enmeshed loyalties, nor hapless love. *He is a man, and that for him and many is sufficient tragedy.* It is not an irritating accident that the tone of the poem is so high and its theme so low. It is the theme in its deadly seriousness that begets the dignity of tone: "lif is læne: eal scæceð leoht and lif somod [life is transitory: all light and life depart together]." So deadly and ineluctable is the underlying thought, that those who in the circle of light, within the besieged hall, are absorbed in work or talk and do not look to the battlements, either do not regard it or recoil. Death comes to the feast, and they say He gibbers: He has no sense of proportion.

I would suggest, then, that the monsters are not an inexplicable blunder of taste; they are essential, fundamentally allied to the underlying ideas of the poem, which give it its lofty tone and high seriousness. The key to the fusion-point of imagination that produced this poem lies, therefore, in those very references to Cain which have often been used as a stick to beat an ass—taken as an evident sign (were any needed) of the muddled heads of early Anglo-Saxons. They could not, it was said, keep Scandinavian bogies and the Scriptures separate in their puzzled brains. The New Testament was beyond their comprehension. I am not, as I have confessed, a man so diligent as duly to read all the books about

Beowulf, but as far as I am aware of the most suggestive approach to this point appears in the essay *Beowulf and the Heroic Age* to which I have already referred. I will quote a small part of it.

> In the epoch of *Beowulf* a Heroic Age more wild and primitive than that of Greece is brought into touch with Christendom, with the Sermon on the Mount, with Catholic theology and ideas of Heaven and Hell. We see the difference, if we compare the wilder things—the folk-tale element—in *Beowulf* with the wilder things of Homer. Take for example the tale of Odysseus and the Cyclops—the No-man trick. Odysseus is struggling with a monstrous and wicked foe, but he is not exactly thought of as struggling with the powers of darkness. Polyphemus, by devouring his guests, acts in a way which is hateful to Zeus and the other gods: yet the Cyclops is himself god-begotten and under divine protection, and the fact that Odysseus has maimed him is a wrong which Poseidon is slow to forgive. But the gigantic foes whom *Beowulf* has to meet are identified with the foes of God. Grendel and the dragon are constantly referred to in language which is meant to recall the powers of darkness with which Christian men felt themselves to be encompassed. They are the "inmates of Hell," "adversaries of God," "offspring of Cain," "enemies of mankind." Consequently, the matter of the main story of *Beowulf,* monstrous as it is, is not so far removed from common mediaeval experience as it seems to us to be from our own. . . . Grendel hardly differs from the fiends of the pit who were always in ambush to waylay a righteous man. And so Beowulf, for all that he moves in the world of the primitive Heroic Age of the Germans, nevertheless is almost a Christian knight.

There are some hints here which are, I think, worth pursuing further. Most important is it to consider how and why the monsters become "adversaries of God," and so begin to symbolize (and ultimately to become identified with) the powers of evil, even while they remain, as they do still remain in *Beowulf,* mortal denizens of the material world, in it and of it. I accept without argument throughout the attribution of *Beowulf* to the "age of Bede"—one of the firmer conclusions of a department of research most clearly serviceable to criticism: inquiry into the probable date of the effective composition of the poem as we have it. So regarded *Beowulf* is, of course, an historical document of the first order for the study of the mood and thought of the period and one perhaps too little used for the purpose by professed historians. But it is the mood of the author, the essential cast of his imaginative apprehension of the world, that is my concern, not history for its own sake; I am interested in that time of fusion only as it may help us to understand the poem. And in the poem I think we may observe not confusion, a half-hearted or a muddled business, but a fusion that has occurred *at a given point* of contact between old and new, a product of thought and deep emotion.

One of the most potent elements in that fusion is the Northern courage: the theory of courage, which is the great contribution of early Northern literature. This is not a military judgement. I am not asserting that, if the Trojans could have employed a Northern king and his companions, they would have driven Agamemnon and Achilles into the sea, more decisively than the Greek hexameter routs the alliterative line—though it is not improbable. I refer rather to the central position the creed of unyielding will holds in the North. With due reserve we may turn to the tradition of pagan imagination as it survived in Icelandic. Of English pre-Christian mythology we know practically nothing. But the fundamentally similar heroic temper of ancient England and Scandinavia cannot have been founded on (or perhaps rather, cannot have generated) mythologies divergent on this essential point. "The Northern Gods," Ker said, "have an exultant extravagance in their warfare which makes them more like Titans than Olympians; *only they are on the right side, though it is not the side that wins. The winning side is Chaos and Unreason*"—mythologically the monsters—"*but the gods, who are defeated, think that defeat no refutation.*" And in their war men are their chosen allies, able when heroic to share in this "absolute resistance, perfect because without hope." At least in this vision of the final defeat of the humane (and of the divine made in its image), and in the essential hostility of the gods and heroes on the one hand and the monsters on the other, we may suppose that pagan English and Norse imagination agreed.

But in England this imagination was brought in touch with Christendom, and with the Scriptures. The process of "conversion" was a long one, but some of its effects were doubtless immediate: an alchemy of change (producing ultimately the mediaeval) was at once at work. One does not have to wait until all the native traditions of the older world have been replaced or forgotten; for the minds which still retain them are changed, and the memories viewed in a different perspective: *at once they become more ancient and remote, and in a sense darker.* It is through such a blending that there was available to a poet who set out to *write* a poem—

and in the case of *Beowulf* we may probably use this very word—on a scale and plan unlike a minstrel's lay, both new faith and new learning (or education), and also a body of native tradition (itself requiring to be learned) for the changed mind to contemplate together. The native "learning" cannot be denied in the case of *Beowulf*. Its display has grievously perturbed the critics, for the author draws upon tradition at will for his own purposes, as a poet of later times might draw upon history or the classics and expect his allusions to be understood (within a certain class of hearers). He was in fact, like Virgil, learned enough in the vernacular department to have an historical perspective, even an antiquarian curiosity. He cast his time into the long-ago, because already the long-ago had a special poetical attraction. He knew much about old days, and though his knowledge—of such things as sea-burial and the funeral pyre, for instance—was rich and poetical rather than accurate with the accuracy of modern archaeology (such as that is), one thing he knew clearly: those days were heathen—heathen, noble, and hopeless.

But if the specifically Christian was suppressed, so also were the old gods. Partly because they had not really existed, and had been always, in the Christian view, only delusions or lies fabricated by the evil one, the *gastbona,* to whom the hopeless turned especially in times of need. Partly because their old names (certainly not forgotten) had been potent, and were connected in memory still, not only with mythology or such fairy-tale matter as we find, say, in *Gylfaginning,* but with active heathendom, religion and *wigweorþung* [sacrifice to idols]. Most of all because they were not actually essential to the theme.

The monsters had been the foes of the gods, the captains of men, and within Time the monsters would win. In the heroic siege and last defeat men and gods alike had been imagined in the same host. Now the heroic figures, the men of old, *hæleð under heofenum,* remained and still fought on until defeat. For the monsters do not depart, whether the gods go or come. A Christian was (and is) still like his forefathers a mortal hemmed in a hostile world. The monsters remained the enemies of mankind, the infantry of the old war, and became inevitably the enemies of the one God, *ece Dryhten,* the eternal Captain of the new. Even so the vision of the war changes. For it begins to dissolve, even as the contest on the fields of Time thus takes on its largest aspect. The tragedy of the great temporal defeat remains for a while poignant, but ceases to be finally important. It is no defeat, for the end of the world is part of the design of Metod, the Arbiter who is above the mortal world. Beyond there appears a possibility of eternal victory (or eternal defeat), and the real battle is between the soul and its adversaries. So the old monsters became images of the evil spirit or spirits, or rather the evil spirits entered into the monsters and took visible shape in the hideous bodies of the *þyrsas* [demons] and *sigelhearwan* [Ethiopians] of heathen imagination.

But that shift is not complete in *Beowulf*—whatever may have been true of its period in general. Its author is still concerned primarily with *man on earth*, rehandling in a new perspective an ancient theme: that man, each man and all men, and all their works shall die. A theme no Christian need despise. Yet this theme plainly would not be so treated, but for the nearness of a pagan time. The shadow of its despair, if only as a mood, as an intense emotion of regret, is still there. The worth of defeated valour in this world is deeply felt. As the poet looks back into the past, surveying the history of kings and warriors in the old traditions, he sees that all glory (or as we might say "culture" or "civilization") ends in night. The solution of that tragedy is not treated—it does not arise out of the material. We get in fact a poem from a pregnant moment of poise, looking back into the pit, by a man learned in old tales who was struggling, as it were, to get a general view of them all, perceiving their common tragedy of inevitable ruin, and yet feeling this more *poetically* because he was himself removed from the direct pressure of its despair. He could view from without, but still feel immediately and from within, the old dogma: despair of the event, combined with faith in the value of doomed resistance. He was still dealing with the great temporal tragedy, and not yet writing an allegorical homily in verse. Grendel inhabits the visible world and eats the flesh and blood of men; he enters their houses by the doors. The dragon wields a physical fire, and covets gold not souls; he is slain with iron in his belly. Beowulf's *byrne* [corselet] was made by Weland, and the iron shield he bore against the serpent by his own smiths: it was not yet the breastplate of righteousness, nor the shield of faith for the quenching of all the fiery darts of the wicked.

Almost we might say that this poem was (in one direction) inspired by the debate that had long been held and continued after, and that it was one of the chief contributions to the controversy: shall we or shall we not consign the heathen ancestors to perdition? What good will it do posterity to read the battles of Hector? "Quid Hinieldus cum Christo? [What does Hinieldus have to do with Christ?]" The author of *Beowulf* showed forth the permanent value of that *pietas* which treasures the memory of man's struggles in the dark past, man fallen and not yet saved, disgraced but not dethroned. It would seem to have been part of the English temper in its strong sense of tradition, dependent doubtless on dynasties, noble houses, and their code of honour, and strengthened, it may be, by the more inquisitive and less severe Celtic learning, that it should, at least in some quarters and despite grave and Gallic voices, preserve much from the Northern past to blend with Southern learning, and new faith.

It has been thought that the influence of Latin epic, especially of the *Aeneid,* is perceptible in *Beowulf,* and a necessary explanation, if only in the exciting of emulation, of the development of the long and studied poem in early England. There is, of course, a likeness in places between these greater and lesser things, the *Aeneid* and *Beowulf,* if they are read in conjunction. But the smaller points in which imitation or reminiscence might be perceived are inconclusive, while the real likeness is deeper and due to certain qualities in the authors independent of the question whether the Anglo-Saxon had read Virgil or not. It is this deeper likeness which makes things, that are either the inevitabilities of human poetry or the accidental congruences of all tales, ring alike. We have the great pagan on the threshold of the change of the world; and the great (if lesser) Christian just over the threshold of the great change in his time and place: the backward view: "multa putans sortemque animo miseratus iniquam [thinking many things and pitying in his soul the hostile fate/chance]."

But we will now return once more to the monsters, and consider especially the difference of their status in the Northern and Southern mythologies. Of Grendel it is said: *Godes yrre bær* [He bore God's ire]. But the Cyclops is god-begotten and his maiming is an offence against his begetter, the god Poseidon. This radical difference in mythological status is only brought out more sharply by the very closeness of the similarity in conception (in all save mere size) that is seen, if we compare *Beowulf* (740ff.) with the description of the Cyclops devouring men in *Odyssey,* 9—or still more in *Aeneid,* 3 (622ff.). In Virgil, whatever may be true of the fairy-tale world of the Odyssey, the Cyclops walks veritably in the historic world. He is seen by Aeneas in Sicily, *monstrum horrendum, informe, ingens* [a dreadful sight, unformed, huge], as much a perilous fact as Grendel was in Denmark, "earmsceapen on weres wæstmum . . . næfne he wæs mara þonne ænig man oðer [a wretched one in the form of a man . . . except that he was greater than any other man]"; as real as Acestes or Hrothgar.

At this point in particular we may regret that we do not know more about pre-Christian English mythology. Yet it is, as I have said, legitimate to suppose that in the matter of the position of the monsters in regard to men and gods the view was fundamentally the same as in later

Icelandic. Thus, though all such generalizations are naturally imperfect in detail (since they deal with matter of various origins, constantly reworked, and never even at most more than partially systematized), we may with some truth contrast the "inhumanness" of the Greek gods, however anthropomorphic, with the "humanness" of the Northern, however titanic. In the Southern myths there is also rumour of wars with giants and great powers not Olympian, the "Titania pubes fulmine deiecti [Titanian youths who were cast down by the thunderbolt]," rolling like Satan and his satellites in the nethermost Abyss. But this war is differently conceived. It lies in a chaotic past. The ruling gods are not besieged, not in ever-present peril or under future doom. Their offspring on earth may be heroes or fair women; it may also be the other creatures hostile to men. The gods are not the allies of men in their war against these or other monsters. The interest of the gods is in this or that man as part of their individual schemes, not as part of a great strategy that includes all good men, as the infantry of battle. In Norse, at any rate, the gods are within Time, doomed with their allies to death. Their battle is with the monsters and the outer darkness. They gather heroes for the last defence. Already before euhemerism saved them by embalming them, and they dwindled in antiquarian fancy to the mighty ancestors of Northern kings (English and Scandinavian), they had become in their very being the enlarged shadows of great men and warriors upon the walls of the world. When Baldr is slain and goes to Hel he cannot escape thence any more than mortal man.

This may make the Southern gods more godlike—more lofty, dread, and inscrutable. They are timeless and do not fear death. Such a mythology may hold the promise of a profounder thought. In any case it was a virtue of the Southern mythology that it could not stop where it was. It must go forward to philosophy or relapse into anarchy. For in a sense it had shirked the problem precisely by not having the monsters in the centre—as they are in *Beowulf* to the astonishment of the critics. But such horrors cannot be left permanently unexplained, lurking on the outer edges and under suspicion of being connected with the Government. It is the strength of the Northern mythological imagination that it faced this problem, put the monsters in the centre, gave them victory but no honour, and found a potent but terrible solution in naked will and courage. "As a working theory absolutely impregnable." So potent is it, that while the older Southern imagination has faded for ever into literary ornament, the Northern has power, as it were, to revive its spirit even in our own times. It can work, even as it did work with the *goðlauss* viking, without gods: martial heroism as its own end. But we may remember that the poet of *Beowulf* saw clearly: the wages of heroism is death.

For these reasons I think that the passages in *Beowulf* concerning the giants and their war with God, together with the two mentions of Cain (as the ancestor of the giants in general and Grendel in particular) are specially important.

They are directly connected with Scripture, yet they cannot be dissociated from the creatures of Northern myth, the ever-watchful foes of the gods (and men). The undoubtedly scriptural Cain is connected with *eotenas* [giants] and *ylfe* [elves], which are the *jötnar* and *álfar* of Norse. But this is not due to mere confusion—it is rather an indication of the precise point at which an imagination, pondering old and new, was kindled. At this point new Scripture and old tradition touched and ignited. It is for this reason that these elements of Scripture alone appear in a poem dealing of design with the noble pagan of old days. For they are precisely the elements which bear upon this theme. Man alien in a hostile world, engaged in a struggle which he cannot win while the world lasts, is assured that his foes are the foes also of Dryhten, that his courage noble in itself is also the highest loyalty: so said thyle and clerk.

In *Beowulf* we have, then, an historical poem about the pagan past, or an attempt at one—literal historical fidelity founded on modern research was, of course, not attempted. It is a poem by a learned man writing of old times, who looking back on the heroism and sorrow feels in them something permanent and something symbolical. So far from being a confused semi-pagan—historically unlikely for a man of this sort in the period—he brought probably *first* to his task a knowledge of Christian poetry, especially that of the Cædmon school, and especially Genesis. He makes his minstrel sing in Heorot of the Creation of the earth and the lights of Heaven. So excellent is this choice as the theme of the harp that maddened Grendel lurking joyless in the dark without that it matters little whether this is anachronistic or not. *Secondly,* to his task the poet brought a considerable learning in native lays and traditions: only by learning and training could such things be acquired, they were no more born naturally into an Englishman of the seventh or eighth centuries, by simple virtue of being an "Anglo-Saxon," than ready-made knowledge of poetry and history is inherited at birth by modern children.

It would seem that, in his attempt to depict ancient pre-Christian days, intending to emphasize their nobility, and the desire of the good for truth, he turned naturally when delineating the great King of Heorot to the Old Testament. In the *folces hyrde* [peoples' guardian] of the Danes we have much of the shepherd patriarchs and kings of Israel, servants of the one God, who attribute to His mercy all the good things that come to them in this life. We have in fact a Christian English conception of the noble chief before Christianity, who could lapse (as could Israel) in times of temptation into idolatry. On the other hand, the traditional matter in English, not to mention the living survival of the heroic code and temper among the noble households of ancient England, enabled him to draw differently, and in some respects much closer to the actual heathen *hæleð,* the character of Beowulf, especially as a young knight, who used his great gift of *mægen* to earn *dom* and *lof* among men and posterity.

Beowulf is not an actual picture of historic Denmark or Geatland or Sweden about A.D. 500. But it is (if with certain minor defects) on a general view a self-consistent picture, a construction bearing clearly the marks of design and thought. The whole must have succeeded admirably in creating in the minds of the poet's contemporaries the illusion of surveying a past, pagan but noble and fraught with a deep significance— a past that itself had depth and reached backward into a dark antiquity of sorrow. This impression of depth is an effect and a justification of the use of episodes and allusions to old tales, mostly darker, more pagan, and desperate than the foreground.

To a similar antiquarian temper, and a similar use of vernacular learning, is probably due the similar effect of antiquity (and melancholy) in the *Aeneid*—especially felt as soon as Aeneas reaches Italy and the "Saturni gentem . . . sponte sua veterisque dei se more tenentem. Ic þa leode wat ge wið feond ge wið freond fæste worhte, æghwæs untæle ealdc wisan [the race of Saturn . . . preserving itself by its own accord and by the will of the old god. I know that your people both with friend and enemy are firmly disposed, in every respect blameless in the old way]." Alas for the lost lore, the annals and old poets that Virgil knew, and only used in the making of a new thing! The criticism that the important matters are put on the outer edges misses this point of artistry, and indeed fails to see why the old things have in *Beowulf* such an appeal: it is the poet himself who made antiquity so appealing. His poem has more value in consequence, and is a greater contribution to early mediaeval thought than the harsh and intolerant view that consigned all the heroes to the devil. We may be thankful that the product of so noble a temper has been preserved by chance (if such it be) from the dragon of destruction.

The general structure of the poem, so viewed, is not really difficult to perceive, if we look to the main points, the strategy, and neglect the many points of minor tactics. We must dismiss, of course, from mind the notion that *Beowulf* is a "narrative poem," that it tells a tale or intends to tell a tale sequentially. The poem "lacks steady advance": so Klaeber heads a critical section in his edition. But the poem was not meant to advance, steadily or unsteadily. It is essentially a balance, an opposition of ends and beginnings. In its simplest terms it is a contrasted description of two moments in a great life, rising and setting; an elaboration of the ancient and intensely moving contrast between youth and age, first achievement and final death. It is divided in consequence into two opposed portions, different in matter, manner, and length: A from 1 to 2199 (including an exordium of 52 lines); B from 2200 to 3182 (the end). There is no reason to cavil at this proportion; in any case, for the purpose and the production of the required effect, it proves in practice to be right.

This simple and *static* structure, solid and strong, is in each part much diversified, and capable of enduring this treatment. In the conduct of the presentation of Beowulf's rise to fame on the one hand, and of his kingship and death on the other, criticism can find things to question, especially if it is captious, but also much to praise, if it is attentive. But the only serious weakness, or apparent weakness, is the long recapitulation: the report of Beowulf to Hygelac. This recapitulation is well done. Without serious discrepancy it retells rapidly the events in Heorot, and retouches the account; and it serves to illustrate, since he himself describes his own deeds, yet more vividly the character of a young man, singled out by destiny, as he steps suddenly forth in his full powers. Yet this is perhaps not quite sufficient to justify the repetition. The explanation, if not complete justification, is probably to be sought in different directions.

For one thing, the old tale was not first told or invented by this poet. So much is clear from investigation of the folk-tale analogues. Even the legendary association of the Scylding court with a marauding monster, and with the arrival from abroad of a champion and deliverer was probably already old. The plot was not the poet's; and though he has infused feeling and significance into its crude material, that plot was not a perfect vehicle of the theme or themes that came to hidden life in the poet's mind as he worked upon it. Not an unusual event in literature. For the contrast—youth and death—it would probably have been better, if we had no journeying. If the single nation of the *Geatas* had been the scene, we should have felt the stage not narrower, but symbolically wider. More plainly should we have perceived in one people and their hero all mankind and its heroes. This at any rate I have always myself felt in reading

Beowulf; but I have also felt that this defect is rectified by the bringing of the tale of Grendel to Geatland. As Beowulf stands in Hygelac's hall and tells his story, he sets his feet firm again in the land of his own people, and is no longer in danger of appearing a mere *wrecca,* an errant adventurer and slayer of bogies that do not concern him.

There is in fact a double division in the poem: the fundamental one already referred to, and a secondary but important division at line 1887. After that the essentials of the previous part are taken up and compacted, so that all the tragedy of Beowulf is contained between 1888 and the end. But, of course, without the first half we should miss much incidental illustration; we should miss also the dark background of the court of Heorot that loomed as large in glory and doom in ancient Northern imagination as the court of Arthur: no vision of the past was complete without it. And (most important) we should lose the direct contrast of youth and age in the persons of Beowulf and Hrothgar which is one of the chief purposes of this section: it ends with the pregnant words "oþ þæt hine yldo benam mægenes wynnum, se þe oft manegum scod [until old age deprived him of strength's delights, he who often injured many]."

In any case we must not view this poem as in intention an exciting narrative or a romantic tale. The very nature of Old English metre is often misjudged. In it there is no single rhythmic pattern progressing from the beginning of a line to the end, and repeated with variation in other lines. The lines do not go according to a tune. They are founded on a balance; an opposition between two halves of roughly equivalent phonetic weight, and significant content, which are more often rhythmically contrasted than similar. They are more like masonry than music. In this fundamental fact of poetic expression I think there is a parallel to the total structure of *Beowulf. Beowulf* is indeed the most successful Old English poem because in it the elements, language, metre, theme, structure, are all most nearly in harmony. Judgement of the verse has often gone astray through listening for an accentual rhythm and pattern: and it seems to halt and stumble. Judgement of the theme goes astray through considering it as the narrative handling of a plot: and it seems to halt and stumble. Language and verse, of course, differ from stone or wood or paint, and can be only heard or read in a time-sequence; so that in any poem that deals at all with characters and events some narrative element must be present. We have none the less in *Beowulf* a method and structure that within the limits of the verse-kind approaches rather to sculpture or painting. It is a composition not a tune.

This is clear in the second half. In the struggle with Grendel one can as a reader dismiss the certainty of literary experience that the hero will not in fact perish, and allow oneself to share the hopes and fears of the Geats upon the shore. In the second part the author has no desire whatever that the issue should remain open, even according to literary convention. There is no need to hasten like the messenger, who rode to bear the lamentable news to the waiting people (2892ff.). They may have hoped, but we are not supposed to. By now we are supposed to have grasped the plan. Disaster is foreboded. Defeat is the theme. Triumph over the foes of man's precarious fortress is over, and we approach slowly and reluctantly the inevitable victory of death.

"In structure," it was said of *Beowulf*, "it is curiously weak, in a sense preposterous," though great merits of detail were allowed. In structure actually it is curiously strong, in a sense inevitable, though there are defects of detail. The general design of the poet is not only defensible, it is, I think, admirable. There may have previously existed stirring verse dealing in straightforward manner and even in natural sequence with Beowulf's deeds, or with the fall of Hygelac; or again with the fluctuations of the feud between the houses of Hrethel the Geat and Ongentheow the Swede; or with the tragedy of the Heathobards, and the treason that destroyed the Scylding dynasty. Indeed this must be admitted to be practically certain: it was the existence of such connected legends—connected in the mind, not necessarily dealt with in chronicle fashion or in long semi-historical poems—that permitted the peculiar use of them in *Beowulf*. This poem cannot be criticized or comprehended, if its original audience is imagined in like case to ourselves, possessing only *Beowulf* in splendid isolation. For *Beowulf* was not designed to tell the tale of Hygelac's fall, or for that matter to give the whole biography of Beowulf, still less to write the history of the Geatish kingdom and its downfall. But it used knowledge of these things for its own purpose—to give that sense of perspective, of antiquity with a greater and yet darker antiquity behind. These things are mainly on the outer edges or in the background because they belong there, if they are to function in this way. But in the centre we have an heroic figure of enlarged proportions.

Beowulf is not an "epic," not even a magnified "lay." No terms borrowed from Greek or other literatures exactly fit: there is no reason why they should. Though if we must have a term, we should choose rather "elegy." It is an heroic-elegiac poem; and in a sense all its first 3,136 lines are the prelude to a dirge: "him þa gegiredan Geata leode ad ofer eorðan unwaclicne [there for him the people of the Geats made ready a splendid funeral pile on the earth]": one of the most moving ever written. But for the universal significance which is given to the fortunes of its hero it is an enhancement and not a detraction, in fact it is necessary, that his final foe should be not some Swedish prince, or treacherous friend, but a dragon: a thing made by imagination for just such a purpose. Nowhere does a dragon come in so precisely where he should. But if the hero falls before a dragon, then certainly he should achieve his early glory by vanquishing a foe of similar order.

There is, I think, no criticism more beside the mark than that which some have made, complaining that it is monsters in both halves that is so disgusting; one they could have stomached more easily. That is nonsense. I can see the point of asking for *no* monsters. I can also see the point of the situation in *Beowulf.* But no point at all in mere reduction of numbers. It would really have been preposterous, if the poet had recounted Beowulf's rise to fame in a "typical" or "commonplace" war in Frisia, and then ended him with a dragon. Or if he had told of his cleansing of Heorot, and then brought him to defeat and death in a "wild" or "trivial" Swedish invasion! If the dragon is the right end for Beowulf, and I agree with the author that it is, then Grendel is an eminently suitable beginning. They are creatures, *feond mancynnes* [mankind's enemies], of a similar order and kindred significance. Triumph over the lesser and more nearly human is cancelled by defeat before the older and more elemental. And the conquest of the ogres comes at the right moment: not in earliest youth, though the nicors are referred to in Beowulf's *geogoðfeore* [time of youth] as a presage of the kind of hero we have to deal with; and not during the later period of recognized ability and prowess; but in that first moment, which often comes in great lives, when men look up in surprise and see that a hero has unawares leaped forth. The placing of the dragon is inevitable: a man can but die upon his death-day.

I will conclude by drawing an imaginary contrast. Let us suppose that our poet had chosen a theme more consonant with "our modern judgement"; the life and death of St Oswald. He might then have made a poem, and told first of Heavenfield, when Oswald as a young prince against all hope won a great victory with a remnant of brave men; and then have passed at once to the lamentable defeat of Oswestry, which seemed to destroy the hope of Christian Northumbria; while all the rest of Oswald's life, and the traditions of the royal house and its feud with that of Deira might be introduced allusively or omitted. To anyone but an historian in search of facts and chronology this would have been a fine thing, an heroic-elegiac poem greater than history. It would be much better than a plain narrative, in verse or prose, however steadily advancing. This mere arrangement would at once give it more significance than a straightforward account of one king's life: the contrast of rising and setting, achievement and death. But even so it would fall far short of *Beowulf.* Poetically it would be greatly enhanced if the poet had taken violent liberties with history and much enlarged the reign of Oswald, making him old and full of years of care and glory when he went forth heavy with foreboding to face the heathen Penda: the contrast of youth and age would add enormously to the original theme, and give it a more universal meaning. But even so it would still fall short of *Beowulf.* To match his theme with the rise and fall of poor "folk-tale" Beowulf the poet would have been obliged to turn Cadwallon and Penda into giants and demons. It is just because the main foes in *Beowulf* are inhuman that the story is larger and more significant than this imaginary poem of a great king's fall. It glimpses the cosmic and moves with the thought of all men concerning the fate of human life and efforts; it stands amid but above the petty wars of princes, and surpasses the dates and limits of historical periods, however important. At the beginning, and during its process, and most of all at the end, we look down as if from a visionary height upon the house of man in the valley of the world. A light starts— "lixte se leoma ofer landa fela [the light of (the hall) glittered over many lands]"—and there is a sound of music; but the outer darkness and its hostile offspring lie ever in wait for the torches to fail and the voices to cease. Grendel is maddened by the sound of harps.

And one last point, which those will feel who today preserve the ancient *pietas* towards the past: *Beowulf* is not a "primitive" poem; it is a late one, using the materials (then still plentiful) preserved from a day already changing and passing, a time that has now forever vanished, swallowed in oblivion; using them for a new purpose, with a wider sweep of imagination, if with a less bitter and concentrated force. When new *Beowulf* was already antiquarian, in a good sense, and it now produces a singular effect. For it is now to us itself ancient; and yet its maker was telling of things already old and weighted with regret, and he expended his art in making keen that touch upon the heart which sorrows have that are both poignant and remote. If the funeral of Beowulf moved once like the echo of an ancient dirge, far-off and hopeless, it is to us as a memory brought over the hills, an echo of an echo. There is not much poetry in the world like this; and though *Beowulf* may not be among the very greatest poems of our Western world and its tradition, it has its own individual character, and peculiar solemnity; it would still have power had it been written in some time or place unknown and without posterity, if it contained no name that could now be recognized or identified by research. Yet it is in fact written in a language that after many centuries has still essential kinship with our own, it was made in this land, and moves in our northern world beneath our Northern sky, and for those who are native to that tongue and land, it must ever call with a profound appeal—until the dragon comes.

The World of the Poem

T. A. Shippey

Any text, prose or poetry, carries much more information within it than its creator realized or intended. What was implicit knowledge for the poet and his Anglo-Saxon audience may need to be made explicit for us, and the possibility that one's judgements are ethnocentric has always to be reckoned with. Just the same, many of the poet's beliefs and prejudices are downright familiar, and others respond to analysis. The essential caveat is that the framework within which judgements are made needs to be set up before fine literary details are filled in. Good readers have probably always done this, consciously or unconsciously; bad readers have approached the poem already burdened with their own hypothetical *Scyldingids*.

Words and Meaning

A single scene will do to document these assertions—that of Beowulf's arrival in Denmark and his challenge by the coastguard (ll. 229–300), a scene which turns on an evident if unacknowledged crux. What has happened so far is that we have been introduced to the Danish royal dynasty, the Scyldings; have seen the present king, Hrothgar, build the great hall of Heorot; and have then been told how Grendel, "the mighty spirit," haunts it and kills its inhabitants. The news reaches Beowulf, still named only as "Hygelac's thane"; he chooses his men and sets sail for Denmark. But as soon as he arrives, this speedy progress is checked by the Danish coastguard, who rides down and, in the poem's first

From *Beowulf.* © 1978 by T. A. Shippey. Edward Arnold Ltd., 1978.

passage of direct speech, asks the hero who he is. Beowulf replies, still without revealing his name, but giving his father's and stating his business. The coastguard then begins his next speech with a brief maxim or aphorism:

> Æghwæþres sceal
> scearp scyldwiga gescad witan,
> worda ond worca, se þe wel þenceð.
> (287–89)

Translating this ought not to be difficult. *Æghwæþer* can mean "each" or "every," and *gescad* comes from a root meaning to divide, or separate, or decide, so there is a little semantic play in the concepts, but hardly very much. The latest published rendering (Howell D. Chickering's text and translation of 1977) has: "A keen-witted shield-bearer who thinks things out carefully must know the distinction between words and deeds, keep the difference clear." This is syntactically accurate. However, it makes no sense. Any fool can tell the difference between words and deeds, and Beowulf's deeds anyway turn out much the same as his words. What can the coastguard mean?

The problem here is caused by the fact that proverbs are not merely linguistic phenomena. We know this from our own experience, since we habitually use formulas which are entirely tautologous ("Business is business") or on a literal level meaningless ("Don't cross your bridges till you come to them"), without feeling any block in communication at all. The hidden factor is the extralinguistic frame; we have been taught in childhood when to use proverbs, what their metaphors mean, who to say them to, and how to take them. It is this nonverbal knowledge that we need to be able to understand the coastguard's "gnome." Reluctance to reconstruct such intangibles and dogged staring at "the text" have led literary critics only into controversy. Thus one scholar decided that the words were just a pompous way for the coastguard to say *he* was a keen-witted shield bearer; another thought they were a kind of apology; a third takes them as grudging deference ("I suppose you know what you are talking about"); naturally they have been seen as conveying involved and subtle moral lessons. In fact the answer is not especially obscure; but to reach it one must consider not the maxim alone, but the maxim in social and dramatic context.

Strong clues to its purport have already been given by the cautious balancing of both the coastguard's initial challenge and Beowulf's subsequent reply. Superficially the coastguard is threatening: he does not dismount, he waves a spear, the first thing he says is "Who are you?" The *second* thing he says, though, is his job: "I have long been the frontier guard, kept watch over the sea." So his questions are not idle or unofficial. He goes on to state the reasons why he ought to be suspicious, and also why his suspicions might be allayed: Beowulf and his men have come openly and without permission (innocence or defiance?), one of them is of imposing physique and appearance (danger or reassurance?). Only after these balanced clauses does he repeat his demand to know who the intruders are, and then he does it with possibly studied impersonality: "haste is best," he says, not "you had better hurry."

In his speech one might well feel that, though no threat has been expressed, there is one somewhere nearby. That seems exactly what the situation calls for. The coastguard is prepared to use words like "pirates" and "spies" (*scipherge, leassceaweras*), and recognizes that even Beowulf's noble bearing may belie him. Violence therefore remains a necessary option. At the same time he keeps these potential insults in the subjunctive, not applying them openly till the chance of peace has been ruled out. Tact and firmness are the Dane's most evident qualities. To this Beowulf replies with something like submissiveness, though not apology: he explains his business, but twice invites the coastguard to correct him if he has been misinformed—"give us good advice"(269), "you will know if things are indeed as we have heard said" (272–73). When he declares his intention of helping the Danes to fight Grendel, he does so for once with reasonable humility, spending six lines on the possibility that he will fail. Beowulf and the coastguard, in short, make signals to each other of mutual respect, taking care to adopt the appropriate roles of Official Inspector (not Personal Challenger), Modest Petitioner (rather than Officious Volunteer). The question of dominance is not raised. Both speeches exude the wary politeness of a society in which men habitually go armed.

And then the coastguard has to make up his mind, which he does immediately after quoting his maxim. Yet the situation *has not changed*. The newcomers have no passports; though one of them has spoken nicely it is without corroboration; the risk of piracy must still be there. In this context the two lines of traditional saying express two different awarenesses—one, that doubt remains, for words are all that have passed, and "deeds speak louder than words"; that just the same decision cannot be shirked, for "needs must when the devil drives." It is the duty of a sharp shield warrior to decide correctly, even on inadequate evidence. "He must be able to judge *everything,* words *as well as* deeds." That is what the maxim says, and the coastguard follows it immediately by doing the right thing and letting the newcomers pass with a firmly "performative" verb, "Ic þæt gehyre," "I hear that this warband is friendly to the lord of the Danes." He backs his judgement to the length of allowing them to keep their weapons and offering to look after their boat.

The scene and the saying form an excellent example of heroic good manners. Naturally we need to adjust our socially determined notions of politeness to understand both properly. It is hard to resist the conclusion, furthermore, that the poet was appealing to a taste already formed. The exchanges with the coastguard and Wulfgar the doorward immediately following are, after all, redundant to the story as a whole; we could have been taken to the intersection between Beowulf and Heorot much more briskly. Their inclusion suggests that the poet knew his audience would relish displays of oral and aural skills from the characters, and would also expect to use such skills themselves (for the coastguard's saying is true generally as well as in context, and could be taken as warning listeners to weigh words wisely too).

However, the main difficulty they present for readers brought up on novels is that they are overwhelmingly "superficial": meaning has to be decoded from words and deeds alone (just as in real life), with only the slightest indications of *thought*. One may well wonder whether this is true of *Beowulf* all the time. Is there any sense in it of discrepancy between the inner character and the outer social role?

Characters and Emotions

One can see straight away that the poet has a sharp eye for discrepancy between actions and feelings. After Beowulf has made his boast that he will fight weaponless against Grendel, he disarms and lies down to sleep in Heorot. In a tableau of heroic propriety his thanes follow suit, surrounding their lord in sleep as they ought to in battle: "around him many a bold sea-warrior turned to his bed in the hall" (689–90). But with the image established, the poet instantly penetrates it:

> Nænig heora þohte, þæt he þanon scolde
> eft eardlufan æfre gesecean,
> folc oþðe freoburh, þær he afeded wæs;
> ac hie hæfdon gefrunen, þæt hie ær to fela micles
> in þæm winsele wældeað fornam,
> Denigea leode.

(Not one of them thought that he would ever leave again in search of his loved home, the noble place and people where he was brought up; but they had heard that in that winehall violent death had taken far too many of the Danish people.)

(691–96)

His aside does not shatter the tableau, but adds to it a silent stoicism. Still, it shows the poet recognizing that his characters *have* feelings. Does he, however, possess the vocabulary to take inner analysis much further? There are examples which suggest that he has not.

The only things we are told directly about the coastguard's state of mind, for instance, are that he was unafraid (287), and actuated by curiosity (232). When he saw the shields and armour coming over the gangplank, "hine fyrwyt bræc" "curiosity urged him in his thoughts, what these men were." But this phrase is used twice more in the poem, once in line 1985, when Beowulf's king Hygelac asks him how he coped with Grendel—"curiosity urged him (*hyne fyrwet bræc*)"—and once in line 2784. This follows the death of the dragon, when Wiglaf robs its treasures and takes them back to the dying Beowulf, so he can leave life easier:

Ar wæs on ofoste, eftsiðes georn,
frætwum gefyrðred; hyne fyrwet bræc,
hwæðer collenferð cwicne gemette.

(The messenger was in haste, eager to get back, speeded by his treasures; curiosity urged him, whether the bold man would find [Beowulf] alive.)

(2783–85)

"Curiosity" seems a callous word here. "Anxiety" would be better, but that would not fit the completely relaxed enquiry of Hygelac, or even the tense but fearless figure of the coastguard. The poet is using one word to cover mental states we would think perceptibly different—a habit which occasionally leads to deeper confusion.

Hreow, for example, is the Old English ancestor of "rue," and normally has associations of regret or penitence. In *Beowulf*, though, it is used once to describe Hrothgar's reaction to the killing of Æschere by Grendel's mother (2129), and once of Beowulf's reaction to the dragon burning his hall (2328). In both cases it is hard to see how "distress" can be taken as far as "penitence," and there is a suspicion that the poet cannot distinguish *hreow* from the etymologically unconnected adjective *hreoh*, "fierce, disturbed," a word used repeatedly by itself and in compounds to describe the very similar mixture of anger and pain felt by kings and heroes and monsters when they are hurt (see lines 1307, 2132, 2296, etc.). In any case the poet uses *wælreow*, "fierce and deadly," with evident approbation at line 629, *blodreow*, "fierce and bloody," with equally evident dislike in line 1719. The semantic field of *hreow/hreoh* between them seems too broad for exactness, while there is equally little useful distinction between any of the poet's frequent words for "sad" and "sorrow"—*wræc, torn, breco*, and the rest. Characters' feelings are intense, for they "burn" and "boil" and "seethe"; but they are not sharply discriminated.

Yet there are half a dozen places in the poem where we are asked to dwell on complex mental progressions, some of them seemingly close to the story's central theme. Many critics feel that the speech of Hrothgar between lines 1700 and 1784 encapsulates the moral of the poem, and its centre is in turn an account of a sinner's development. For some eleven lines Hrothgar describes the root of sin in success, in the physical happiness and freedom of a lucky man, like Beowulf. The result, he says, is that:

> he þæt wyrse ne con—,
> oð þæt him on innan   oferhygda dæl
> weaxeð ond wridað.

> (He does not know the worse—till inside him great arrogance grows and spreads.)
>
> (1739–41)

And having said so much Hrothgar moves rapidly on to allegory—the guardian of the soul, the enemy nearby shooting his arrows, the sinner overcome by diabolic promptings. The "rake's progress" continues with a picture of avarice and envy, visible results of inner failure. But what *was* the inner failure? Are arrogance and prosperity *inevitably* connected? What is "the worse," and what the "bitter arrow" that strikes the sleeping soul? Modern criticism is naturally drawn to explicate these questions, and we would like very much to know as well why Beowulf makes no reply to the whole speech, and whether he sees any connection between it and the calamity which falls on him at the end of his days. When the dragon comes, is his suspicion that he has offended God justified? At that later moment all the poet can say of his hero is:

breost innan weoll
þeostrum geþoncum,   swa him geþywe ne wæs.

(His heart surged internally with dark thoughts, as was not
his custom.)

(2331–32)

Meanwhile Hrothgar's "great arrogance grows and spreads" offers no
＿ ＿＿＿ than his very similar account of Heremod's fall

re grew fierce and

–"arrogance" and

r (weaxeð, wridað,

t the bits of infor-

nse from proverbs

he poet recognizes

ocial role, his pre-

cal, and his morals

to tangibility. It is

suddenly by action

grief at line 1877,

(he could not re-

ught between rage

væfre mod forhab-

n itself within his

mihte ða forhabban

dark thoughts" end

ke this as anything

but right and proper, like the heroic lack of introspection which the poet
tells us is his normal state. In the same way the important fact about
Beowulf's thanes in Heorot is that, whatever they thought, they stayed
by their leader. Their inner pessimism then only does them credit, just
as, a hundred lines later (794–805), their overoptimistic hacking at Grendel is in no sense made foolish by the fact that blades could not harm
him. The poet reserves the right to say what people are thinking; he does
not, however, regard this as ultimately important.

MONEY, WORTH, PRESTIGE

In view of the stress on external factors already noted, it is no surprise to find in the heroes of Beowulf a streak of hard materialism. Money

hardly appears in the poem; the common Old English word for it, *feoh*, is used by itself three times, but on two of these occasions is immediately qualified by phrases meaning "ancient treasures," which show that the word carries its vaguer sense of "valuables." Yet lack of cash does not preclude a continuing interest in payment from both employers and employed. As soon as Hrothgar hears of Beowulf's arrival he says he will give him treasures for his boldness; his last words before leaving the hero to face Grendel are a promise of lavish reward; he says exactly the same thing to persuade Beowulf to pursue Grendel's mother. Even Wealhtheow feels she has to reinforce her pathetic appeal for help with promises (1220, 1225–26): "I will remember your reward. . . . I will give you many treasures." Duty, gratitude, and vengefulness are all present as motives for action, but it is assumed that they have to have tangible support. As for Beowulf, he accepts what he is given, and shows considerable concern about retaining it. When he gets ready to dive into the monsters' lake (1474–91) he thinks first of his men, but second of his property: if he dies, Hrothgar must send it to his next of kin.

All natural enough, we might think. However, we should be careful not to let modern reverence for "economic reality" brainwash us into cynicism. Though Beowulf is careful to collect his winnings, he shows little interest in keeping them. Thus, after Grendel's defeat Hrothgar pays him as bounty a golden banner, a helmet, sword, and mail shirt, eight horses (one of them saddled), with two gold bracelets and a torque from Wealhtheow. (He also gives something to each of the thanes, and remembers to pay compensation for Hondscio, whom Grendel killed.) The poet still has these objects in mind over a thousand lines later (2152–76), when Beowulf gives nearly all of them away again—four horses and all the military objects to Hygelac, three horses and the torque to Hygd. His sole profit from Grendel appears to be one saddled horse and two bracelets. Admittedly Hygelac gives him a sword in return and "seven thousand (hides?)," that is, a province to rule, but maybe as one of only two Geatish princes he could have expected that anyway. One might note that Beowulf also misses an easy chance of profit when he returns from Grendel's hall with a head and a sword hilt and no other treasures at all, "though he saw many there." Why are both he and the poet simultaneously so interested in valuables and so stirred by the thought of giving them away? The answer lies in those bugbears of translation, *lof* and *dom*, "honour," "glory," "praise."

Everyone has noticed the importance of these concepts in the poem. Beowulf himself says that people ought to gain glory before death (*domes*

breost innan weoll
þeostrum geþoncum,   swa him geþywe ne wæs.

(His heart surged internally with dark thoughts, as was not
his custom.)

(2331–32)

Meanwhile Hrothgar's "great arrogance grows and spreads" offers no
more eventual sustenance than his very similar account of Heremod's fall
twenty lines before: "Yet in his mind his heart's treasure grew fierce and
bloody." The nouns and adjectives are clear enough—"arrogance" and
"dark" and "fierce and bloody." The verbs, however (*weaxeð, wridað,
weoll*), remain opaque.

Complaining about this, or straining too hard at the bits of information offered, is as mistaken as trying to wring sense from proverbs
through verbal analysis alone. The fact is that though the poet recognizes
sensibly that people have an existence outside their social role, his pre-
occupations are overwhelmingly moral, not psychological, and his morals
are based on decisions, results, matters which rise to tangibility. It is
therefore characteristic for dilemmas to be dissipated suddenly by action
or by gesture. Hrothgar is caught between love and grief at line 1877,
and weeps; "he þone breostwylm forberan ne mehte (he could not re-
strain the impulse of his heart)." Hengest earlier is caught between rage
and promise, and breaks out in murder; "ne meahte wæfre mod forhabban in hreþre (the restless spirit could not contain itself within his
heart)." When he saw his lord in pain, Wiglaf too "ne mihte ða forhabban
(could not then hold back)." As for Beowulf, his "dark thoughts" end
wordlessly in preparing his armour; it is hard to take this as anything
but right and proper, like the heroic lack of introspection which the poet
tells us is his normal state. In the same way the important fact about
Beowulf's thanes in Heorot is that, whatever they thought, they stayed
by their leader. Their inner pessimism then only does them credit, just
as, a hundred lines later (794–805), their overoptimistic hacking at Grendel is in no sense made foolish by the fact that blades could not harm
him. The poet reserves the right to say what people are thinking; he does
not, however, regard this as ultimately important.

MONEY, WORTH, PRESTIGE

In view of the stress on external factors already noted, it is no surprise to find in the heroes of *Beowulf* a streak of hard materialism. Money

hardly appears in the poem; the common Old English word for it, *feoh*, is used by itself three times, but on two of these occasions is immediately qualified by phrases meaning "ancient treasures," which show that the word carries its vaguer sense of "valuables." Yet lack of cash does not preclude a continuing interest in payment from both employers and employed. As soon as Hrothgar hears of Beowulf's arrival he says he will give him treasures for his boldness; his last words before leaving the hero to face Grendel are a promise of lavish reward; he says exactly the same thing to persuade Beowulf to pursue Grendel's mother. Even Wealhtheow feels she has to reinforce her pathetic appeal for help with promises (1220, 1225–26): "I will remember your reward. . . . I will give you many treasures." Duty, gratitude, and vengefulness are all present as motives for action, but it is assumed that they have to have tangible support. As for Beowulf, he accepts what he is given, and shows considerable concern about retaining it. When he gets ready to dive into the monsters' lake (1474–91) he thinks first of his men, but second of his property: if he dies, Hrothgar must send it to his next of kin.

All natural enough, we might think. However, we should be careful not to let modern reverence for "economic reality" brainwash us into cynicism. Though Beowulf is careful to collect his winnings, he shows little interest in keeping them. Thus, after Grendel's defeat Hrothgar pays him as bounty a golden banner, a helmet, sword, and mail shirt, eight horses (one of them saddled), with two gold bracelets and a torque from Wealhtheow. (He also gives something to each of the thanes, and remembers to pay compensation for Hondscio, whom Grendel killed.) The poet still has these objects in mind over a thousand lines later (2152–76), when Beowulf gives nearly all of them away again—four horses and all the military objects to Hygelac, three horses and the torque to Hygd. His sole profit from Grendel appears to be one saddled horse and two bracelets. Admittedly Hygelac gives him a sword in return and "seven thousand (hides?)," that is, a province to rule, but maybe as one of only two Geatish princes he could have expected that anyway. One might note that Beowulf also misses an easy chance of profit when he returns from Grendel's hall with a head and a sword hilt and no other treasures at all, "though he saw many there." Why are both he and the poet simultaneously so interested in valuables and so stirred by the thought of giving them away? The answer lies in those bugbears of translation, *lof* and *dom*, "honour," "glory," "praise."

Everyone has noticed the importance of these concepts in the poem. Beowulf himself says that people ought to gain glory before death (*domes ær deaþe*) (1388). The poet agrees that "a man will prosper in every nation through *lofdædum,* praiseworthy deeds" (24–25). To modern ears, trained to consider "glory hunting" discreditable, all this sounds ominous, and many have felt that the last word of the poem contains silent reproof, as the Geats say of Beowulf that he was:

> manna mildust   ond monðwærust,
> leodum liðost   ond lofgeornost.

(The mildest of men and the gentlest, the kindest to his people, and most eager for praise.)

(3181–82)

However, the careful and unusual symmetry of the two lines suggests that all four adjectives are meant to be in harmony; the difficulty is no more serious than the nervousness over *druncen* discussed earlier. Acceptance of *lof* and *dom* as absolute goods is nevertheless by no means inconsistent, within the value scheme of the poem, with a strong interest in "portable property."

Consider Beowulf's treatment of the coastguard as he returns from Heorot:

> He þæm batwearde   bunden golde
> swurd gesealde,   þæt he syðþan wæs
> on meodubence   maþme þy weorþra,
> yrfelafe.

(He gave that boat ward a sword bound with gold, so that because of the treasure, the inherited relic, he was from then on *weorþra* on the mead bench.)

(1900–1903)

Weorþra is the comparative form of the word that descends to modern English as "worthy." However, one could hardly say that the man was "worthier" on the mead bench; his character is not changed by the present at all. One might say that he was "worth more," and that would be financially true, but of course not all that is intended. The real point is that the coastguard is more highly esteemed as a result of owning the weapon: it gives him status. And this equation of honour and ownership is entirely characteristic of the poem. When Beowulf receives his first four gifts from Hrothgar, the poet remarks "he had no need to feel shame before warriors at the treasure he was given" (1025–26), and evidently means that people would respect Beowulf just because of his possessions.

Wulfgar the doorward also assumes that fine feathers make fine birds, for he tells Hrothgar that his new visitors seem worthy of esteem "from their warlike equipment (*on wiggetawum*)" (368). The poet consistently lets characters make an impression through their weapons, responding with unfailing admiration to gleaming helmets, bright shields, stacked spears, linked and shining mail. But his reaction is only partly materialistic: the objects are offered as an index of honour, inner worth.

All this explains why *lof* in practice covers "generosity" as well as praise; also why the poem has no use for money (which, being neutral, convertible, and with a value permanently fixed, can tell you nothing about status); and maybe why Beowulf does not bother to pick up Grendel's treasure (since it has not been awarded to him, it has about the same value as a *bought* Victoria Cross, not negligible, but not complete either). As for the hero's spendthrift homecoming, obviously if possession of valuables is a proof of merit, one of the most honourable things you can do is advertise your resources by giving them away! The poet sees virtue in lavish donation as well as reception, and thinks it his job to record both:

> Swa manlice   mære þeoden,
> hordweard hæleþa   heaþoræsas geald
> mearum ond madmum,   swa hy næfre man lyhð,
> se þe secgan wile   soð æfter rihte.

(In this noble way the famous lord, treasure guardian of heroes, paid for the battle charges with horses and precious things, as no man will ever deny—no man who means to tell truth properly.)

(1046–49)

A consistent fusion of tangible and intangible is built into the poem's scenery as into its words. Though the poet never says straight out that "glory," "worth," "treasure," and "weapons" are all aspects of the same thing, his phraseology does the job for him: Beowulf is *dome gewurþad* at line 1645, just as Hrothgar's saddle is *since gewurþad* at 1038 and the "hallman" (a tinge of scepticism here) *wæpnum gewurþad,* "made to look worthy by weapons" at 331. Translation must inevitably be cultural as well as semantic. It is worth noting, though, that this complex of evaluations is not as alien as it might look. Over the last couple of centuries modern English has been busily developing the word "prestige." This meant originally "illusion," but shifted during the nineteenth century in the direction of "influence or reputation derived from previous character . . . or *esp.* from past successes" (so says the *Oxford English Dictionary* entry, published in 1909). Now, of course, it has become something possessed by men of power and (unlike honour) conferred very largely by the trappings of success—the "prestigious" car, clothes, wristwatch, home address. As such it has strong links with *dom* and *lof.* Admittedly, Mr Gladstone in 1878 called "prestige" a "base-born thing" and said specifically that it was not to be used in translating ancient epics. However, being "high-minded" probably spoils more criticism than being "base-born." The word is a useful reminder of the way abstracts and objects can mix.

SWORDS, HALLS, AND SYMBOLS

We are liable to call such mixtures "symbolism." Indeed, according to the *OED* a symbol is "something that stands for, represents, or denotes something else . . . *esp.* a material object representing or taken to represent something immaterial or abstract." The coastguard's sword is a symbol, then, a material object which everyone takes to represent the abstraction *weorþ*. However, one can easily imagine a member of Beowulfian society insisting that this is not symbolism at all, just matter-of-fact. "Look" (he might say) "you wear a sword to show you're ready to fight, and people treat you politely because they can *see* you are. Distinguishing between being ready physically (swords), being ready emotionally (courage), and having social status (honour)—that's just splitting hairs! The three things go together, and if you lose any one of them you'll forfeit the other two very soon." To return to modern terminology, there is a cause-and-effect relationship between the object and what it represents (like that between wealth and Rolls-Royces). The sword is an "index" of honour—admittedly a stylized one—rather than a "symbol" *tout pur.*

This is not just a dispute over vocabulary. We need to keep in mind (as I have said already) that social signs in *Beowulf* function systematically, in systems which cannot be entirely, or even largely, the creation of the poet. The literary associations which "symbolism" has acquired tend to blur this perception and hinder appreciation. Swords in *Beowulf,* for instance, evidently have a life of their own. The young retainer Wiglaf draws his as he prepares to help his king in the dragon's den; and the poet stops for twenty lines (2611–30) to remark on the weapon's significance. This one was not donated, but first won in battle and then inherited. Accordingly it is a reflection of the courage shown by Wiglaf's father and (given Anglo-Saxon notions of good breeding) a sign of hereditary worth. In the end it becomes totally identified with its owner's personality, so much so, as E. B. Irving has noted, that it does not *weaken* and he does not *melt*—we would have expected these verbs the other way round.

But what happens if you inherit nothing? Since weapons are indexes of honour and status, deprivation of them becomes doubly unendurable. Beowulf himself imagines a scene (2032–69) in which a sword is worn by someone like Wiglaf who had it from his father; but this is seen by the man from whose father's corpse it was gloriously taken. "Meaht ðu, min wine, mece gecnawan?" asks a troublemaker (Can you, my friend, recognize that sword?). He means, "Are you a man or a mouse?" but neither Beowulf nor the poet bothers to explain this, since everyone knows the next act has to be murder. In exactly the same way the poet feels that the displaying of a sword to Hengest at the climax of the "Finnsburh Episode" (1143–45) will be self-explanatory. To us, as it happens, it is not; but we can see that the object prompts revenge with irresistible force and in total silence. In *Beowulf* objects can communicate whole chains of abstraction and reflection by their presence alone, and in a way felt by poet and audience to be too natural for words.

Some objects in fact reach "mythic" status—most obviously, halls. What the poet thinks about these can be derived most immediately from his run of twenty to thirty compound words for describing them. Halls are for drinking in ("winehall," "beerhall," "meadhall"); they are filled with people ("guesthall," "retainer hall"); in them worth is recognized ("goldhall," "gifthall," "ringhall"). They are also the typical though not the only setting for festivity and for poetry. It is this "loud merriment in hall" (*dream . . . hludne in healle*) which Grendel hears and hates from the beginning, while Hrothgar's poet sings "clear in Heorot" on every one of the three nights Beowulf spends there. What he produces is *healgamen* (the sport [you expect] of halls), and when the Geats look into their gloomy future at the end, the two things they fear to lose are their "prestigious rings (*hringweorðung*)" and the "melody of the harp" which, rather implausibly, used to "wake the warriors" (from their beds on the hall floor, that is, see lines 1237–40). Finally, whether it is from paint or firelight or candles, halls are associated with brightness. Heorot is *goldfah* (gold ornamented), and shines like a beacon: "lixte se leoma ofer landa fela (the light blazed over many lands)." Inside it is decorated with glittering tapestries, "goldfag scinon web after wagum (on the walls the webs shone golden)," while at line 997 the poet calls it simply *þæt beorhte bold* (the bright building). In the end the dragon comes to Beowulf's home "to burn the bright halls (*beorht hofu bærnan*)," and there is a sudden striking image early on of Grendel prowling "the treasure-ornamented hall on the black nights (*sincfage sel sweartum nihtum*)."

Already one can see how the "mythic" interpretations come in. The hall equals happiness equals light. What do the monsters which invade halls equal? They are creatures of the night, "shadow-walkers," "lurkers in darkness," things which have to be under cover by dawn. It is no great stretch of the imagination to link their darkness with death. Meanwhile the poet's vocabulary, once more, shows an assumption that the happiness of the hall means life. In line 2469 old King Hrethel "gumdream ofgeaf (gave up the joys of men)," his grandson Beowulf (3020–21), "laid aside laughter, *gamen ond gleodream*, merriment and the joys of song," the Last Survivor's kinsmen (2252) "gave up this life, *gesawon seledream*, had seen the joy of the hall." The compound words show how tightly men and harps and halls cluster together in the poet's mind, and presumably in his audience's. A similar familiarity informs the untranslated and possibly unconscious metaphor near the end, when the poet ruminates that it is a mystery where we all must go:

> þonne leng ne mæg
> mon mid his magum   meduseld buan.

(When a man can no longer, with his kinsmen, inhabit the meadhall.)

(3064–65)

Meduseld is semantically indistinguishable from its familiar precursors *medoærn, medoheal*. By this time, however, what it means is "Life-Gone-By." The poet has no need to explain.

Halls are "indexes" of happiness, then, because in them people are most likely to be free from poverty. They are "symbols" too, because they are crowded with not entirely realistic conventional signs, like harps and gold and brightness. Their vulnerability implies a shared social myth about the limits of human capacity (stated most overtly by the councillor of King Edwin in Bede). However, they remain at all times stubborn and solid facts, things which could be seen in reality as well as heard about in poetry. It is important that literal-minded Anglo-Saxons could always take halls literally, because what they would get from *Beowulf* was not the notion that Heorot was like life, but the more searching one that life was like Heorot. "We too," they might conclude, "live in a little circle of light. Every time we go to sleep expecting to wake up, we could be as wrong as Hrothgar's retainers. Æschere is us." Involvement of this nature deepens many of the scenes in the poem. Modern readers no longer reach it naturally and wordlessly, but they are not completely immune to it either. Professor Tolkien's "Golden Hall" in the second volume of *The Lord of the Rings* is still called "Meduseld," and the name still has its power.

ALLUSION AND REALITY

The ethics, behaviour, and vocabulary of Beowulfian characters all hang together, create strong *vraisemblance*. Of course the poet also delights in deliberate fantasy, in things which never happened and never could—the blade melting in Grendel's corrosive blood, the robber stepping cautiously past the sleeping dragon's head, the monsters' dream of banquet on the sea bottom. Most famous perhaps is Hrothgar's evocation of that classic motif of horror story, the animal whose instincts perceive something that human senses cannot. Though the hunted hart may come to the edge of the ominous mere, he says:

> ær he feorh seleð,
> aldor on ofre,   ær he in wille,
> hafelan beorgan;   nis þæt heoru stow!

(Rather will he give up his life and spirit on the shore than plunge in to save his head; it is an uncanny spot!)

(1370–72)

And yet even this fantasia is obeying a fundamental principle of realistic fiction: it implies a depth of memory for Hrothgar to draw on, creatures and landscapes which exist outside the poem's needs, and consequently a weight of fact which urges the reader to think "this must be true." One wonders how much of the poem's impression of realism is as artificially created.

Consider the poem's most redundant character, Yrmenlaf. He appears only in line 1324, as Hrothgar reacts rather crossly to Beowulf's unfortunate "Have you had a pleasant night?" "Don't ask about pleasure," he says. "Sorrow is renewed for the Danish people. Dead is Æschere, Yrmenlaf's elder brother, my confidant, my counsellor, who stood at my shoulder." In the poem Æschere himself functions only as corpse, and it shows a certain conscientiousness on the part of the poet to award him six and a half lines of elegy, as he does. But why bring in his *younger brother*? Is this realism again—the outright invention of corroborating detail? Or is it a sudden appeal to a frame of knowledge existing outside the poem, in which Yrmenlaf was a sort of Pellinore or Bedivere of Danish legend—not a prominent person, but one known to exist?

Obviously no one can say, and it hardly matters, since in that context invention and reminder would work just about as well. However, our uncertainty over Yrmenlaf's very existence dramatizes a series of linked and vital questions of a much more general kind. Is the world of *Beowulf* a never-never land created by the poet? Did the original audience know a version of history into which *Beowulf* had to fit? Most important of all, did the poet *and* his original audience feel that the characters in the poem were in essence men like themselves, or did they see them as irrevocably different, fictional creatures of an imaginary society? Answers to these questions cannot be simple.

There are three immediate reasons, though, for taking a broadly "fictive" and "distanced" view. Nearly all critics agree that the poet must have been a literate Christian Englishman. But if you judged from internal evidence alone you might conclude that he had never been to Britain; had never heard of Christ; and was not exactly sure what "writing" meant. These statements need some qualification. There *is* an Englishman in the poem, that Offa (he gets a mention in lines 1944–62) who according to *Widsith* "ruled the English" (*weold Ongle*)." However, *Widsith* also makes clear that Offa lived near the Eider in Schleswig-Holstein; he "ruled the English" before they migrated to England. Similarly, though the poem contains no books, it does use the verb *writan*. But this seems to mean "cut" not "write." Beowulf "forwrote" the worm (2705), that is, he cut it in two. When the poet says of the giant sword hilt "on it was *writen* the origin of that far-off fight," he may mean it had a picture "engraved" on it. The *runstafas* of line 1695 (are they "secret staves" or "runic letters"?) only spell out the maker's name. As for *scrifan* (modern German *schreiben*), it means "judge, sentence, condemn." The absence of references to Christ is even more puzzling, for it coexists with repeated references to God, the devil, the Flood, Cain and Abel. There can be no doubt that the poet *did* know about Christ, and England, and book learning; his omission of all three indicates a consciousness of anachronism between his own time and that of his story.

Yet in other respects the poet and the characters are very closely identified. It may not seem so at first, for right at the beginning we can feel the narrator seizing control. *He* is the man who knows what is happening across the sea, in the future, in the darkness or within men's hearts. Connecting causes and effects comes naturally to him (see line 7), while he does not find even God's purposes inscrutable (see lines 13–17). The narrator, in brief, knows nearly everything and nearly everybody. When he uses the adjective *nathwylc*, literally "I-know-not-which," it is evident that he also means "and the information is of no importance"; "some slave or other" stole the dragon's gold and "some man or other" hid it in the first place. And yet this near-omniscience comes over as only a developed form of a quality which many men are expected to share, and to which the narrator thinks he can make occasional appeal. Wulfgar appears momentarily, and the narrator observes that his courage and wisdom were "known to many (*manegum gecyðed*); Beowulf says his father was called Ecgtheow, and "many a wise man on earth still remembers him." They may both be wrong, of course, but they are inviting corroboration or contradiction from somewhere. Hrothgar's encyclopaedic knowledge, meanwhile, rivals the narrator's; *he* remembers Ecgtheow, shows traces of prophetic ability, confidently detects the intentions of God. His courtiers show exactly the same comparative tendencies as the poet, for just as the latter says again and again that he has never heard of a greater treasure or a more lavish ship burial or friendlier donations, so the racing thanes say there is no better man than Beowulf, and enshrine their opinion in impromptu verse. It would, indeed, be merely dull not to recognize that the *cyninges þegn* of line 867 is a "disguised narrator." (This concept is explained by Wayne C. Booth, *The Rhetoric of Fiction*.) What he says is what the poet wants us to know, and several of the imagined speakers in *Beowulf* have exactly the same direct but undramatic role—most obviously Hrothgar in lines 1700–1784, the Last Survivor (2247–66), the anonymous Messenger (2900–3027). It is no wonder that no one in the poem responds to any of those speeches, nor that the poet on occasion ticks them overtly as correct—*he ne leag fela wyrda ne worda* (he was not far wrong in words or of events), or in other words "that bit can be relied on."

The narrator and his characters create what amounts to a continuum—the poem of *Beowulf* at one end, at the other nameless gossip like that about Offa's taming of his queen:

> ealodrincende   oðer sædan,
> þæt hio leodbealewa   læs gefremede.

(The beer drinkers told a different tale, that she performed fewer outrages on her people.)

(1945–46)

Between the two lies an entire and well-imagined complex of legendary tradition arising out of contemporary judgement. Of course this could all be a trick—a device of the Flaubertian "poet" who is silently surveying the universe of "narrator" and "characters" without ever appearing in it. But it seems more plausible to think the image is in essence true. The poet after all repeatedly equates truth and poetry through the words *soþ* and *riht* (see lines 871, 1049, 2107–10), and begins by including his audience with himself in the *we* of *Beowulf*'s first two lines: "Listen, we have heard of the might of the kings of the Spear-Danes in ancient days." Again no one can say for sure that these informed listeners are not imaginary too! But they fit in well with the poet's projected image of himself and his characters. Behind them all lies an expanse of legendary tradition, not an abstract force but one repeatedly incarnated in figures like the *ealodrincende,* or the "old land-guardian" of line 1702, who "remembers everything" and "advances truth and right among the people"—a culture bearer, a poet in embryo, a link between real present and just-as-real past.

All this is not to decry the author's originality, nor the very great scope he allows to fiction and to fantasy. Like the hunted hart, the Danish coastguard and Æschere's brother and quite possibly Beowulf himself are born from his imagination into the clear but bounded light of legendary poetry. Nevertheless, it looks as if neither the poet nor his audience would tolerate anything that contradicted too sharply history as they already knew it, while though the world of the poem is no doubt stylized, its social and physical furniture are not merely personal inventions. Most important, we can reasonably suspect that the poet and his audience felt "continuity," if not identity, with dead heroes. They knew all these things happened "long ago (*on geardagum*)," and that "in those days (*þy dogore*)" (1797) some things were different. On the other hand, even in history an eternal stability ruled men and seasons "as it does still (*swa he nu gen deð*)" (1058, 1134, 2859). Furthermore, when the poet says approvingly of Wulfgar "he knew court custom (*cuþe he duguðe þeau*)" (359), clearly he does not mean that *particular* court's custom, he means everybody's. Learning and geography change, we might conclude, but in *Beowulf* etiquette at least is felt to remain fixed and standard.

The *Beowulf* Poet's Sense of History

Roberta Frank

> *I don't know how humanity stands it with a painted paradise at the end of it*
> *without a painted paradise at the end of it*
>
> EZRA POUND, Canto 74

Awareness of historical change, of the pastness of a past that itself has depth, is not instinctive to man; there is nothing natural about a sense of history. Anthropologists report that the lack of historical perspective is a feature of primitive thought, and historians that its absence characterizes medieval thinking: Herod in the Wakefield Cycle swears "by Mahoun in heaven," the medievel Alexander is a knight, and heathen Orléans boasts a university. Morton Bloomfield has shown that a sense of history, even a tentative, underdeveloped one, was a rare thing in fourteenth-century England, and that Chaucer's attention to chronology and his preoccupation with cultural diversity have affinities with aspects of the early Italian Renaissance. But what in the Anglo-Saxon period stimulated a monastic author to stress the differences between ancient days and his own, to paint the past as if it were something other than the present? The *Beowulf* poet's reconstruction of a Northern heroic age is chronologically sophisticated, rich in local color and fitting speeches. The poet avoids obvious anachronisms and presents such an internally consistent picture of Scandinavian society around A.D. 500 that his illusion of historical truth has been taken for the reality.

From *The Wisdom of Poetry: Essays in Early English Literature in Honor of Morton W. Bloomfield,* edited by Larry D. Benson and Siegfried Wenzel. © 1982 by the Board of Trustees of the Medieval Institute. Western Michigan University, Medieval Institute Publishers, 1982.

The poet's heroic age is full of men both "emphatically pagan and exceptionally good," men who believe in a God whom they thank at every imaginable opportunity. Yet they perform all the pagan rites known to Tacitus, and are not Christian. The temporal distance between past and present, acknowledged in the opening words of the poem—*in geardagum* (in days of yore)—is heard again when Beowulf, as yet unnamed, makes his entrance. He is the strongest of men *on þæm dæge þysses lifes* (on that day of this life) (ll. 197, 790). The alliterating demonstratives stress the remoteness of the past, here and later when a hall servant in Heorot looks after all the visitors' bedtime needs "swylce þy dogore heaþoliðende habban scoldon" (such as in those days seafarers were wont to have) (1797–98). The descriptive clause distances but also glosses over, shadowing with vagueness an unknown corner of the past. The poet is so attracted by the aristocratic rituals of life in the hall, so intent on historical verisimilitude, that he imagines everything, even basic human needs, to have changed over time. His proposition that golden tapestries hanging in the hall were a wondrous sight for the partying sixth-century retainers is quickly modified in the direction of reality: "þara þe on swylc stara∂" (for those who look upon such things) (996); even in Heorot not all beefy breakers-of-rings in their cups would have had an eye for interior design. The vividness of the past underlines, paradoxically, its distance.

The *Beowulf* poet has a strong sense of cultural diversity, as strong perhaps as Chaucer's. Three times in the "Knight's Tale" Chaucer explains the behavior of characters with the clause *as was tho the gyse*; in "The Legend of Cleopatra" he has Anthony sent out to win kingdoms and honor *as was usance*; and in "The Legend of Lucrece" he notes approvingly that Roman wives prized a good name *at thilke tyme*. The Old English poet maintains a similar perspective. He praises the Geats for their ancient custom of keeping armor and weapons at their sides at all times: "They were always prepared for war, whether at home or in the field, as their lord required" (1246–50). He has Hrothgar admire their steadfastness, the dependability of men who live blameless *ealde wisan* (in the old fashion) (1865). When the dragon's ravages begin, the poet makes the aged Beowulf fear that he has transgressed *ofer ealde riht* (against ancient law) (2330): pagans have their own moral code, separating them from the author and us. The poet emphasizes cultural differences not only between present and past but also between coeval peoples. He depicts the Swedes and Geats as more authentically primitive, more pagan in outlook and idiom, than the Danes. When a roughhewn Beowulf arrives at the Danish court he puts himself in the hands of a skilled local who "knew the custom of the retainers" (359). Ongentheow, the grizzled king of the Swedes, threatens to pierce (*getan*) (2940) captives on the gallows for the pleasure of carrion birds. The Geats consult auspices (204); Beowulf, like the Scandinavian heroes of old, trusts in his own might (418, 670, 1270, 1533); the messenger imagines a raven boasting to an eagle of carnage feasts (3024–27); and Hæthcyn's slaying of Herebeald (2435–43) imitates a fratricide in the Norse pantheon: euhemerism becomes, in the poet's hands, an aid to historical research.

The poet's sense of anachronism is revealed in his characters' speeches, utterances that avoid all distinctively Christian names and terms. The actors themselves have a sense of the past and of the future. They are able to look back two generations, tracing the origins of the feud between the Geats and the Swedes (2379–96, 2472–89, 2611–19, 2379–96). They can also forecast the feuds of the next generation. There is a fine display of chronological wit when Beowulf, on the basis of a piece of information picked up at the Danish court, turns the Ingeld legend into a political prophecy, a sequence of events likely to occur in the near future (2024–69). The poet's sense of historic succession is so strong and the internal chronology of the poem so carefully worked out that his audience knows why Hrothulf and Heoroweard have to be kept in the wings a little while longer. After Beowulf's death, it is clear even to the messenger that Eadgils is not likely to sit for long on the Swedish throne without avenging his brother's murder on the new king of the Geats, son of the slayer. The poet does not make earlier Danish and Germanic heroes like Scyld, Heremod, Finn, Offa, Sigemund, Eormenric, and Hama contemporaneous with the sixth-century events narrated, but sets them in a distant mirror, conveying the illusion of a many-storied long-ago. Such chronological tidiness is all the more remarkable for its appearance in a poetic vernacular that has no distinctive future tense, and whose chief adverbs of recollection and continuation—*þa* and *siððan* (thereupon: looking forward; at that time, from the time that: looking back)—are almost always ambiguous.

Philosophically, in order to have a sense of history at all, the *Beowulf* poet had to hold certain premises about man and his role on earth. Despite his professional concern with the timeless, he had to be engaged to some extent with the things of this world; he needed a positive attitude toward secular wisdom and some notion of natural law. Above all, he had to believe that pagan Germanic legend had intellectual value and interest for Christians. These concepts were available to twelfth-century humanists. Christian Platonists like William of Conches, Bernard Silvestris, and Alan of Lille shared an unpolemical attitude toward the pagan past and stressed the importance of earthly understanding as the base of all human knowledge. But in the central theological traditions of the early medieval West and, more specifically, in the teachings of Aldhelm, Bede, and Alcuin, there is no trace of this liberal mentality. No contemporary of these three concerned himself with man on earth, looking upon heathen virtues and customs with an indulgent eye, and had his vision survive. The patristic tradition that pagan story is diabolically inspired, that unbaptized pagans lie lamenting in hell, was too strong.

Purely from the perspective of the history of ideas, the *Beowulf* poet's chronological acrobatics and fascination with cultural diversity, his positive view of those who lived "while men loved the lawe of kinde," needs explanation. We cannot, wielding editorial knives, remove these ideas from the text the way other late-seeming growths have been excised solely on the grounds that the poem is early. "It is a dangerous principle to adopt in literary investigation that nothing we do not readily understand can be rationally explained. We must as a working principle assume that everything in a work of art is capable of explanation even at the cost of oversubtlety and even error. . . . We must not assume, unless we are finally forced to it, that the writer or composer did not know what he was doing." Professor Bloomfield offered this guidance in a review of Kenneth Sisam's *The Structure of Beowulf*. Sisam contends that "great difficulties stand in the way of all explanations that make the poet a deep thinker, attempting themes and ways of conveying them that might be tried on a select body of readers in a more advanced age." The fact remains, however, that the poem, for an early composition, is full of oddly advanced notions. Twenty years ago Morton Bloomfield observed that *ealde riht* (old law) (2330) in *Beowulf* referred not to the Mosaic Code, the Old Law, but to natural law, and noted that the moral laws of the Old Testament were often equated with this natural law, "although in general this equation is later than the early Middle Ages." More recently, he has seen behind Beowulf's single combat with Grendel the concept of the *iudicium Dei,* a calling upon God to decide the justice of an action: "Let wise God, the holy Lord, adjudge the glory to whichever side he thinks fit," says Beowulf (685–87); the champion will rely in the coming struggle on the judgment of God (440–41). Something like the judicial duel appears to have been a feature of medieval Scandinavian society. Yet all the early evidence for trial by combat from Tacitus to Pope Nicholas I is Continental; there is no documentation for multilateral ordeal in England before the Norman Conquest. The *Beowulf* poet's use of the form and spirit of the judicial duel, whether he derived the concept from Tacitus, from the Franks, or from the Danelaw, emphasizes—like his auguries, sacrifices, and exotic cremations—the temporal and cultural distance between the pagan Scandinavian past and the England of his own day. His backward glance is both admiring and antiquarian.

Anglo-Saxon scholarship has done its best to read *Beowulf* as the seventh and eighth centuries would have. Because Aldhelm and Bede insisted that the only suitable subject for poetry was a religious one, and because secular epics and long historical poems only started to appear in the later ninth century, Margaret Goldsmith had little choice but to interpret *Beowulf* allegorically. Alcuin's only known comment on heroic literature in ecclesiastical contexts is an orthodox denunciation of it as a heathen distraction. W. F. Bolton's new book on *Alcuin and Beowulf* discovers, predictably, that the great schoolmaster would have found Beowulf guilty, flawed, vengeful, incapable even of protecting his people. Charles Donahue attempts to account for the existence of an eighth-century Old English poem about noble pagans by invoking Irish views of pre-Christian goodness, legends that tell of virtuous pagans and their natural knowledge of God. Yet the stories of Cormac and Morand that he cites are not easy to date (that of Cormac is surely no earlier than the last quarter of the tenth century), and Donahue concedes that they are "later than *Beowulf* and can be viewed only as parallel developments of that early insular Christian humanism." Patrick Wormald has recently located a social and cultural context for the composition of heroic literature in the aristocratic climate of early English Christianity, in the integration of monastic and royal houses. Yet the aristocratic nature of the early English church is, if anything, more pronounced with the passage of time, reaching a kind of culmination under the successors of Alfred. The "vast zone of silence" Wormald observes existing between Bede and the *Beowulf* poet may be due not only to Bede's fundamentalism but also to the centuries separating the two authors.

When in the Anglo-Saxon period did pagans become palatable? A positive attitude toward the pagans of classical antiquity is visible in translations of the Alfredian period. While the real Orosius, writing in the first decades of the fifth century, was as reluctant as Bede to say anything good about those who lived before the Christian Era, the Old English paraphrase of *Orosius* from around 900 contemplates with pleasure the bravery, honorable behavior, and renown of several early Romans, adds references to Julius Caesar's clemency, generosity, and courage, and even suggests that in some of their customs the Romans of the Christian Era were worse than their pagan ancestors. Unlike his source, the Old English translator does not think in an exclusively religious way: what matters is how rulers of the past served God's purpose, not whether they were Christians or pagans.

Boethius's *Consolation of Philosophy,* translated by King Alfred himself, resorted to pre-Christian human history and to pagan mythology for some fifty illustrations, finding archetypal patterns in the behavior of a Nero or a Hercules just as the *Beowulf* poet locates exemplary models in Heremod and Beowulf. In the late ninth and early tenth centuries, the *Consolation* enjoyed a considerable vogue among Carolingian commentators, at least one of whom, Remigius of Auxerre, Alfred may have used. Alfred thrusts aside much of Remigius's Neoplatonic speculation along with his scientific and theological information, but is quick to insert commentary material having to do with classical myths. He occasionally gives a pagan analogy for a Christian concept, something Alcuin never managed to do. Alfred's story of Orpheus teaches that a man who wishes to see the true light of God must not turn back to his old errors. Boethius's tale of Jupiter overthrowing the giants who warred on heaven is shown by Alfred to reflect—*secundum fidem gentilium*—Nimrod's building of the Tower of Babel and God's subsequent division of tongues. Alfred stresses the underlying truthfulness of Boethius's pagan fables. The details of Hercules taming the Centaurs, burning the Hydra's poisonous heads, and slaying Cacus are skipped, but the myth itself is universalized into a philosophic reflection on life and on the meaning of victory and defeat: good men fight for honor in this world, to win glory and fame; for their deeds, they dwell beyond the stars in eternal bliss. Circe in Alfred's paraphrase is no longer the wicked enchantress of Boethius, but a vulnerable goddess who falls violently in love with Odysseus at first sight; she turns his men into animals only after they, out of homesickness, plot to abandon their lord. Alfred, like the *Beowulf* poet, looks for the moral and psychological laws of things, tries to understand and learn rather than condemn. Only once in his paraphrase does he abandon the world of classical paganism for a Germanic allusion; it is a small step, but full of significance for the future of Old English poetry. He translates Boethius's "Where now are the bones of faithful Fabricius?" as "Where now are the bones of the famous and wise goldsmith Weland?"

When in the Anglo-Saxon period could a Christian author exploit pagan Germanic legend for its intellectual and moral values? Seventh- and eighth-century sources furnish evidence that English monks were overfond of harpists, secular tales, eating, and drinking; but such worldly tastes provoked the scorn and hostility of their superiors: "What has Ingeld to do with Christ? The House is narrow, it cannot hold both. The King of Heaven wishes to have no fellowship with so-called kings, who are pagan and lost." But by the late ninth century, even an archbishop— Fulk of Rheims, who recruited Remigius of Auxerre, corresponded with King Alfred and sent Grimbald to him—could in one and the same sentence refer to a letter of Gregory the Great on kingship and to "Teutonic books regarding a certain King Hermenric." A century and a half later, puritanical youth can be seen shaking its fist at reckless middle age in a letter that one cleric of Bamberg Cathedral wrote to another complaining of their bishop, Gunther, who spent all his time reading of Attila and Theodoric when not composing epics himself.

The *Beowulf* poet insists on the virtue and paganism of his characters, and is unusually explicit about their heathen rites, describing them lovingly and at length. A slender tradition of extolling the good customs of Germanic pagans can be traced in Roman authors, but this tradition does not enjoy a continuous run through the medieval period. The first known use of Tacitus's *Germania* after Cassiodorus occurs in the mid-ninth-century *Translatio Sancti Alexandri* by the monk Rudolf of Fulda. This work, commissioned by the aristocratic abbot of the monastery of Wildeshausen in Saxony, opens with a description of the moral practices and brave deeds of the early pagan ancestors of the Saxons. Bede, monk of Wearmouth-Jarrow and historian of the English church and people (ca. 731), is reticent about the doings of the Anglo-Saxons before their conversion and shows no inclination to celebrate heathens or their habits. Widukind, monk of Corvey and historian of the Continental Saxons (ca. 967), does not hesitate to do so. He borrows Rudolf of Fulda's account of pagan institutions and shapes the heathen past of his nation into a carefully contoured whole. He develops a single thread of historical tradition into a complex narrative, incorporating heroic dialogue, vivid details, and dramatic scenes, in much the same way that the *Beowulf* poet seems to have worked. Widukind saw his efforts in recording the deeds of the Saxon leaders (*principum nostrorum res gestae litteris . . . commendare*) as equal in value to the service he earlier performed with his two lives of saints. He wrote his history, he said, partly by virtue of his monastic calling, partly as a member of *gens Saxonum*. One historical sense seems to beget another: Widukind, like the *Beowulf* poet, learned much from classical historians, including the art of depicting people whose behavior made sense within the framework of their age and culture.

The *Beowulf* poet's attribution of monotheism to his good heathens is sometimes taken as revealing his ignorance of Germanic paganism, sometimes as a sign of his inability to see the past as anything other than the present. Like Widukind, he mentions pagan error, briefly and in passing (175–88), before depicting noble pagan monotheists for some three thousand lines. In the Alfredian *Orosius,* as in the fifth-century original, God is shown to have always guided the world, even in pagan times. But the paraphraser adds a few touches of his own: the pagan Leonidas places his trust in God; even Hannibal is heard to lament that God would not allow him domination over Rome. The *Beowulf* poet, too, makes his heroes refer again and again to the power and providence of a single God, and he takes Beowulf's victory as a sign that "God has always ruled mankind, as he still does" (700–2, 1057–58). The Danes' hymn in Heorot to a single Almighty (90–98) expresses a Boethian wonder at seeing an invisible God through his creation. Wiglaf's contention that the fallen Beowulf shall for a long time "abide in the Lord's keeping" (3109) suggests a Boethian philosophy of salvation, of individuals ascending by reason alone to a knowledge of one God. It was probably Remigius of Auxerre who around 900 compiled a short treatise on the gods of classical antiquity, announcing—in the final paragraph of his prologue—that a single divine being lay behind the multiplicity of Greek and Roman names for the gods. Renewed contact with the texts of late antiquity, especially Macrobius, Martianus Capella, and Boethius, ended by making some men at least think in a less narrowly religious way. The *Beowulf* poet allows glimpses of a *paradiso terrestre* in the distant past— brief, transitory but glowing moments whose thrust is to remind his hearers of all the unfulfilled potential of their pre-Christian heritage.

What emerges from a sufficiently intense concern for history in any literary work is a series of projections inevitably focused by the particular anxieties of the writer. Alfred's *Boethius* reveals that king's fascination with the psychology of the tyrant, his concern for the proper uses of power and wealth, and his insistence, against Boethius, that temporal possessions can be put to good ends. The *Beowulf* poet seems especially concerned to distinguish between justifiable and unjustifiable aggression, to place the warlike activities of his pagan hero in an ethical context. Beowulf resorts to arms out of concern for the defenseless and for the common good, not exclusively out of lust for conquest, ambition, or vengefulness. He is heroic and pious, a pagan prince of peace. Christianity in the early barbarian West may have thought it was being assimilated by a warrior aristocracy, but it ended up—even before the Crusades—

accommodating itself to the heroic values of the nobility. The blending of the two cultures would have begun at the time of conversion, but it was an extended process. At one stage, revelry in the hall, vowing oaths of fidelity to a lord, ambushes and plundering and slaughter, all the duties and responsibilities of heroic society were seen as demonic and damnable, as in the eighth-century *Life of Guthlac* by Felix of Crowland. In the Old English *Guthlac A,* the poet even sends in devils to remind the royal saint and hermit of his secular obligations, to tempt him with the hall delights long abandoned after a warlike youth (191–99). The heroic life is the opposite of the life that leads to salvation.

The synthesis of religious and heroic idealism present in *Beowulf* was probably not available to monastic authors at an early date. In the 930s, Odo of Cluny wrote his *Life of St. Gerald of Aurillac* in order to demonstrate for his own aristocratic circle how a layman and noble lord, a man out in the world, could lead a holy existence. Odo gives moral and religious dimensions to Gerald's lifelong martial career. The warrior soothes the suspicious, squelches the malicious, and puts down the violent who refuse to come to terms; he does this not for personal gain but in order to achieve peace for his society. So Beowulf restrains, one after the other, coastguard, Unferth, and Grendel, making friends of two potential foes and ridding Denmark of monsters who pay no wergild. Ottonian Saxony as portrayed by Widukind is—in the heroic cast of its values and the ferocity of its feuds—very close to the world of *Beowulf.* Tenth-century monastic narratives seem, like *Beowulf,* able to find a place for heroic values—even fighting and the bonds of kinship—within a Christian framework. In Hrotsvitha's *Gongolfus* the ideals of a warrior's life are fused with the Christian goal of *caritas,* while Ruotger's *Life of Bruno,* archbishop of Cologne and brother of Otto the Great, reports with some understatement that "priestly religion and royal determination united their strength" in him. Like these works, the Old English poems that we can date to the tenth century set up no unresolvable contradictions between piety and the heroic life. *The Battle of Maldon,* composed after 991 and regarded as the finest utterance of the Anglo-Saxon heroic age (and most "Germanic" since Tacitus), contains a prayer by a warlord soon to be venerated by the monks of Ely. *The Battle of Brunanburh,* from around 937, is red with blood, God's rising and setting sun, and a historical perspective reminiscent of manifest destiny. *Judith,* probably from the same century, focuses on a prayerful heroine who chops off heads with only slightly less savoir faire than Beowulf. Between *Bede's Death Song* and *Maldon* something happened to Old English poetry, whether we call this something rebarbarization or adapting Christian models for a new and only partly literate secular aristocracy. New syntheses were becoming possible. Unlike Anglian stone crosses of the eighth century, English religious sculpture after the Danish invasions was able to draw, like *Beowulf,* on pagan myth and heroic legend.

In still another area, the vision of the *Beowulf* poet seems to derive from contemporary concerns, from a need to establish in the present an ideological basis for national unity. I suggested in an earlier paper that the *Beowulf* poet's incentive for composing an epic about sixth-century Scyldings may have had something to do with the fact that, by the 890s at least, Heremod, Scyld, Healfdene, and the rest, were taken to be the common ancestors both of the Anglo-Saxon royal family and of the ninth-century Danish immigrants, the *Scaldingi.* The *Beowulf* poet admires kings who, like Hrothgar, have regional overlordship of surrounding tribes and who, like Beowulf, are powerful enough to keep neighbors in check. A key political catchword—*þeodcyning* (great or national king)—is prominently displayed by the poet in his opening sentence. He depicts the Danish nation's former glory in a time when powerful kings had been able to unite the various peoples of the land, something that did not occur with any permanence in Denmark or England until the tenth century. The *Beowulf* poet does his best to attach his pagan champion to as many peoples as possible—Danes, Geats, Swedes, Wulfings, and Wægmundings—as if to make him the more authentically representative of the culture and traditions of central Scandinavia: an archetypal Northman. Epics have their propagandist appeal. There is a relationship, however indirect, between Virgil's account of the majesty of Rome's legendary past, the glory of her ancient traditions, and the Augustan program to bring back a "pristine" patriotism and code of morals. Both the *Aeneid* and *Beowulf* are in some sense historical novels, mythically presented, philosophically committed, and focused on the adventures of a new hero. Both poets project onto the distant past features of the society of their own day, consciously and deliberately, in order to provide a sense of continuity. Virgil's Rome is grounded in an earlier Rome; the *Beowulf* poet anchors the West Saxon *imperium* in a brilliant North Germanic antiquity. By the twelfth century, the Normans were very French; yet the more French they became, the more they stressed their Danish ancestry and the heroic deeds of their founding dynasty. By the first quarter of the tenth century, the Danes in England were working hard to be more Christian and English than the English: at midcentury both archbishops of England, Oda and Oskytel, were of Danish extraction. An Old English poem about northern heathens and northern heroes, opening with the mythical figure of Scyld from whom the ruling houses of both Denmark and England were descended, fits nicely with the efforts of Alfred and his successors to promote an Anglo-Danish brotherhood, to see Dane and Anglo-Saxon as equal partners in a united kingdom.

The sadness, the poignancy, the *lacrimae rerum* we associate with *Beowulf* come from the epic poet's sense of duration, of how "time condemns itself and all human endeavor and hopes." Yet though Heorot is snuffed out by flames and noble pagans and their works perish, the poet does not scorn the heroic fellowship whose passing he has had to tell. There is still something left worth ambition: "The task to be accomplished is not the conservation of the past, but the redemption of the hopes of the past." The last word in the poem is uttered by sixth-century

commend Beowulf as *lofgeornost* (most intent on glory). Lady

that the praise won even by
of a tiny earth is inhabited,
and philosophy; even writ-
d their authors in obscurity.
: point. He argued that the
a kind of *trahison des clercs*—
for heora slæwðe *and* for
riten þara monna ðeawas *and*
and weorðgeornuste wæron"
who—in their sloth and in
written the virtues and deeds
enowned and most intent on
on Bloomfield has often re-
t the deeds of a great man in
d a model." Those of us who
1's students at Harvard know

300 Colorado Street, Suite 200 Austin, TX 78701
512-495-6504

glish poem about northern heathens and northern heroes, opening with
the mythical figure of Scyld from whom the ruling houses of both Denmark and England were descended, fits nicely with the efforts of Alfred
and his successors to promote an Anglo-Danish brotherhood, to see Dane
and Anglo-Saxon as equal partners in a united kingdom.

The sadness, the poignancy, the *lacrimae rerum* we associate with
Beowulf come from the epic poet's sense of duration, of how "time condemns itself and all human endeavor and hopes." Yet though Heorot is
snuffed out by flames and noble pagans and their works perish, the poet
does not scorn the heroic fellowship whose passing he has had to tell.
There is still something left worth ambition: "The task to be accomplished is not the conservation of the past, but the redemption of the
hopes of the past." The last word in the poem is uttered by sixth-century
Geats who commend Beowulf as *lofgeornost* (most intent on glory). Lady
Philosophy assured Boethius (bk. 2, part 7) that the praise won even by
noble souls is of slight value: only a small part of a tiny earth is inhabited,
and by nations differing in language, custom, and philosophy; even written euologies fail because time veils them and their authors in obscurity.
King Alfred did not entirely accept her last point. He argued that the
fame of a great man can also fade through a kind of *trahison des clercs*—
"þurh þa heardsælþa þara writera ðæt hi for heora slæwðe *and* for
gimeleste *and* eac for recceleste forleton unwriten þara monna ðeawas *and*
hiora dæda, þe on hiora dagum formæroste *and* weorðgeornuste wæron"
(through the bad conduct of those writers who—in their sloth and in
carelessness and also in negligence—leave unwritten the virtues and deeds
of those men who in their day were most renowned and most intent on
honor). The purpose of *Beowulf,* as Morton Bloomfield has often reminded us, is heroic celebration, to present the deeds of a great man in
order "to give his audience new strength and a model." Those of us who
were privileged to be Professor Bloomfield's students at Harvard know
what such a model can be worth.

Digressive Revaluation(s)

Raymond P. Tripp, Jr.

A Digression on Digressions

Criticism is necessarily digressive, since paradoxically it keeps us out of literature. Nonetheless, the digressions in *Beowulf* deserve one of their own, aimed at explaining what they are and where they come from. Such questions probably should not even be cast in the plural, since the common feature of all digressions is their digressiveness. A digression remains, for all its putative appositeness, etc., something else than the main story line or "central fable." Yet Leyerle's influential view that "There are no digressions in *Beowulf*" epitomizes the kind of literary treatment they have recently received. Even the earlier studies of Tolkien, of Bonjour, and more recently of Carrigan, have all been directed toward proving that the digressions are not there or have all the time been something else than we thought they were, and so on; in a word, that the poem is not bad because of them. Nonetheless, modern readers sense marked differences of style and story, and want to know why—what to make of these patches of "intricate assimilation of narrative and other materials in the poem." The real questions about digressions in *Beowulf* are not such as whether they exist or not, or how they work in the poet's style, but rather what they are and why they are there. The question of their ultimate artistic merit depends upon one's—epochal—taste.

Much of the controversy surrounding the poet's digressiveness has arisen from the fact that we have not yet discovered or admitted why he digresses in the first place. Our lack of sympathetic understanding is

---

From *More About the Fight with the Dragon:* Beowulf *2208b–3182, Commentary, Edition and Translation.* © 1983 by University Press of America.

likely, moreover, to have more than one cause. Most important, perhaps, is the question of incompatible mentalities and the narrative expectations which arise from them, exacerbated by the perennial problem of careless reading. In any case, the uncritical assumption that the poet's digressions are in fact secondary narratives competing with the main story line has worked great mischief, not least by creating a false problem to be explained away. This tack explains a number of studies which have taken the form of demonstrating that the digressions are not what they are because they "work" in the poet's poem. Such, of course, may point to the poet's talent, but they do not explain why he shows it in digressions. Another more subtle problem is the assumption that a digression, even if it "works" with rather than against the "central fable," must be narrative in nature. The intricacies of the criticism surrounding the poet's digressions could easily fill a book. They all, however, have their roots in the problem of conflicting mentalities—not only between modern readers and the poem, but between the poet—as an earlier modern—and his own traditions.

To substantiate this point one need not wax *weltanschaulich* nor short-circuit demonstration with an appeal to the "history of consciousness." There is plenty of evidence within *Beowulf* itself for a generative epochal conflict of worlds, and for what this predicament does to language and storial matter. Without taking sides on the issue of literature as a reflex of cultural history, one may argue that *Beowulf* studies have swung from one explanatory extreme to another and have recently come to rest in a peculiarly excited eclecticism, often too belletristic to register the element of epochal contrast and its effect upon all aspects of the poem. Contrast has often been recognized as an important force in the poem, but primarily in conscious structural ways. The depth to which the roots of contrast sink into the soil of *Beowulf* has yet to be acknowledged. Yet this element of epochal contrast—between "pagan" and archaic and "Christian" and modern—and its role in the poet's digressive, revaluative style is the key to his redefinition of "bravery" and "action" itself.

The poet's digressiveness, thus, emerges in the context of an increasingly internalized world as the means of registering his new understanding of human action, and telling us what he thinks are the essential facts of life and what men can do about them. In this the *Beowulf* poet is a Milton ahead of his time. It may, of course, be a literary truism that a great poet is one who revalorizes language and culture. But specifically it is through digressing that our poet presents the values and perspectives through which the more actional parts of his poem—what there is of them—are to be understood. Action is, after all, only action. Out of context it is even less—mere motion. Meaningfulness is motion in context. The killing of a dragon is no more than dangerous, until we know how, why, and to what end, and so on. Literary history is full of dragons and heroes who have dispatched them. The *Beowulf* poet must stop, as it were, and tell us in just what way Beowulf's actions are more than a replay of immemorial sequences. He does this in his digressions.

Some of his digressions are like exempla, and this is why they point rather than compete with his tale. The longer ones, of course, exhibit internal narrative structure; but whatever storial force they evince is subsumed, that is, internalized, into its modulating effect upon, in this case, the actual fight with the man-dragon. Because even the longer, storial digressions do not mesh like gears into the machinery of the main plot, there is no need nor really any possibility of "interlacing" them, so to speak. Their relationship to the "central fable," from which actually they may not be extricated, is not structural, but *modal*. Their relevance, further, is not always and narrowly thematic, but often even broader and deeper even than the literary structure in which they participate. They are often part of the world producing the poem as well as part of the world within the poem. They "work" in many ways and directions—sometimes through truncated, radically abbreviated and paradigmatic recapitulations of events, sometimes through existential assertions we call gnomic, sometimes through longer moralizations, sometimes through simple variation, and so on. But no matter what form their digressiveness takes, they "work" to qualify, to redefine the action before the audience, one might say, to desynonymize it from pagan action, so that it will be as clear as possible that this action is not just the same old thing, but something in a new key. In this regard, the *Beowulf* poet's use of "digression" as a technique of redefinition is akin to Chaucer's pervasive use of the figure of *occupatio*. Whenever Chaucer's sources contain recalcitrant material he would expunge, he simply throws the offending part of a story away, with a telltale statement that it's all too long and boring to tell over again. The *Beowulf* poet uses this overt technique but once, when his hero is relating his Danish adventures to Hygelac (ll. 2093–96a). Such digressiveness suggests that it might be well to replace the metaphor of "interlace" with one of "collapse." For in many ways the poem contains numerous "collapsed" narratives, in which, for reasons of that censorship of the past which follows from cultural change, old stories and events are internalized from structural to a modal status. Storial or actional form persists, but its force is lost: it no longer commands its own narrative center, lacks primary significance, and exists in fact only to grace what has now become the real tale. It is this secondary, once removed, and "melted" quality, for which Beowulf's "melted" hall is a fitting emblem, which catches the modern reader's attention, whose inevitabilities are no longer the poet's. This is the main point. The poet's digressions are not to be explained away, so to speak, by "re-interlacing" them again, as if all there were to do were to tie up loose ends, so that they might resume their ancient and transparent life. Living complexities always command an imperative simplicity; we are never aware of "moving parts," that is, until they stop moving as they were designed to. What looks now like a dead patch on living narrative tissue, like a storial infarction, was once doubtless invisible, because the white light of intense convictions and necessities obliterated new suturing. Just as the lover never sees the lines on his mistress's face, a revisionary audience might never have bothered about these things we call digressions. But when we do begin to look with different eyes, then we notice, and this very perception brings them into existence. The *Beowulf* poet digressed because he differed: his world was no longer of his tradition. And we balk, because we differ too.

Cultural change—whether drift, accident, or evolution—creates a succession of mental epochs, and as a result, all English poetry is essentially "metaphysical," since its very substance is the redefinition of values. John Donne was far from being the first to make ideas his subject. Carrigan brings this emphasis upon ideas to bear upon *Beowulf,* asserting that the poet's tendency is "to be concerned with 'themes' or ideas rather than with narrative interest." It does not seem, however, as Carrigan would have it, that "the poet had no choice in the matter," because he was "dominated by words which express the essential qualities rather than the particular elements of things described." It is more likely that his way of looking at things, that is, the revaluative dialectic which arose out of the contrasts this generated, is what accounts for his digressing, as well as the absence of striking visual images; he may be as abstract or theological as he is "essential." A homiletic poet would be more interested in redefining than in merely describing "heroic action." He is too good for his style to be attributed entirely to the aesthetic limitations of his inherited linguistic vehicle. Any poet's language will of itself contribute much to his poetry, and no one is totally free from the language he uses. But a good poet frequently succeeds in turning his limitations into advantages, as the *Beowulf* poet does, especially in his use of archaic "knot" imagery, which he is unravelling into history.

This modal status of digressive narrative leads to an interesting corollary. Insofar as the poet's digressions contain his epochal revaluations, they contain his poetry too. There is where his values and significances—his unique "punch"—resides. Many a critic has recognized this fact, that, somehow, the poem seems written inside out, none more tellingly than W. P. Ker. In his *Epic and Romance,* he found the main story trivial, but the digressions and supporting episodes truly heroic and magnificent. Later, in *The Dark Ages,* he put forward his now famous judgment upon the poem's style:

> The great beauty, the real value . . . is in its dignity of style. In construction it is curiously weak, in a sense preposterous; for while the main story is simplicity itself, the merest commonplace of heroic legend, all about it, in the historic allusions, there are revelations of a whole world of tragedy, plots different in import from that of *Beowulf,* more like the tragic themes of Iceland. Yet within this radical defect, a disproportion that puts the irrelevances in the centre and the serious things on the outer edges, the poem *Beowulf* is unmistakably heroic and weighty. The thing itself is cheap; the moral and the spirit of it can only be matched among the noblest authors.

This, of course, is the criticism of a modern man; it neglects that the *Beowulf* poet was only on his way to becoming modern. The modern view disparages *mere* action, "the merest commonplace of heroic legend," while it prefers the conscious awareness of internalized action, "the moral and the spirit." The mere killing of monsters is less than sensational, mostly efficiently dispatched in a dozen other and better ways than individual combat. This style of criticism finds its counterpart in the disparagement of the hero's behavior, whose bravery is read as bravado and selfishness. But since ideas are what make poetry, at least for modern people, the modern reader often prefers the poet's digressions where act is subsumed by mode.

Another interesting corollary follows from this modal status of the poet's digressions. For when we catch on to what he is doing in them, we can see that *the entire poem is a digression*—some might call it a deviation—from and upon the heroic or epic poem where actions are alive and well, and speak for themselves without the poet's running commentary upon their meaning. Sensing this, George J. Englehardt used the word "dilation." More recently, John C. McGalliard has expressed the pervasiveness of "comment" in the poem. Although he distinguishes between "comment" and "digression," he adds the qualification:

Digressions are outside the scope of this study, but obviously some of them at least may be regarded as comments by the poet developed at such length as to constitute narrative units in themselves.

McGalliard stresses the poet's "fondness for reflective remarks," which Klaeber [in his edition], interestingly enough, doubtless assuming that the poem was an epic and reflection, therefore, out of place, regarded as "apparently uncalled-for ethical reflection." But at times, as McGalliard remarks, "the comment is hardly separable from the narrative." Even more recently, Theodore M. Andersson has qualified *Beowulf* as a "quasi-epic narrative":

> The poet drew his settings from the scenic repertory of the older heroic lay, but he strung these traditional scenes together with a moralizing commentary in the form of digressions, flash-backs, anticipations, authorial remarks, reflective speeches, and a persistent emphasis on unexpected reversals—all tending to underscore the peaks and valleys of human experience.

One might say that the "quasi epic" is a digression upon the primary epic; but it is blended rather than assembled or woven, asserted, i.e., "preached," not told.

And still another, third, corollary following from the poet's digressiveness is that his highly repetitive, "interlaced" syntax and narrative may, surprisingly enough, be modern rather than archaic. The archaic view of reality, including the human body, involved the idea of "weaving" and "tying"—the world is a vast "knot." But "interlace" as we have it in *Beowulf* may be a boundary or inter*face* phenomenon, resulting from the untying of this ancient knot into linear narrative. Those who push the "interlace" metaphor beyond its valid usefulness (of reminding us of the uniqueness of *Beowulfian* narrative) overlook the fact that, even in visual and plastic art, genuinely archaic interlace is symmetrical, traceable, and thus teleological; whereas what we have in *Beowulf* seems thematically juxtapositional, the outcome of collapsed narratives being put to new uses, more according to new meaning, that is, symbolic force, than by shape or pattern beyond an alternating negative-positive narrative dualism. One might risk the metaphor "stalled" or "becalmed" narrative, a style caught in the doldrums between archaic and modern, where little psychic wind is blowing. Repetition may imply problems as well as pleasures. The poet's excessive use of the so-called action marker *þā* [then, thereupon], thus, may signal an almost desperate attempt to communicate his version of the world before the threatening resurgence of the vast tide of archaic narrative he is striving to stem. His recapitulatory return to Beowulf and the king's loss of his hall (2324ff.), for example, does not advance the narrative with new action. We know already the hall is destroyed. The poet is rather *stopping to explain* precisely why Beowulf's anger is not going to be like that of any other pagan king who, as we know from *Maxims I* (58b), *biþ anwealdes georn* (is always eager for sole power). Beowulf is no run-of-the-mill pagan monarch; he is a responsible—one wants to say Christian—king who is angry for his people, not only himself. Repetition, digression, redefinition, "interlace," etc., are, therefore, all interpenetrating forms of modal revaluation of actional narrative, variously informed by radical epochal contrasts. Even the revered kenning, as Thomas Gardner has argued, may not be of ancient German origin, but something of a "Christian import." And "any two-membered substitution for a substantive of common speech" (Meissner) may be the smallest kind of digression. William Whallon's conclusion, further, that kennings are "low in economy," points in the same direction. *Beowulf* is essentially a digressive work, a culture-wide "homily."

Carrigan's restatement of the old problem can be profitably viewed as a sharpening of Ker's original formulation. The digressions contain "the passages of the greatest intensity in the poem." Further, the digressions "possess the enigmatic clarity of image and symbol . . . as symbolic statements of the ideas to become explicit and central." Yet Carrigan is still caught up in the structural at the cost of modal possibilities of the poet's digressiveness, speaking also of "an echoing quality which links them with other digressions and episodes, and finally with the central action of the poem." He does, however, also speak of the "fittingness and inevitability which come[s] from having lain in the poem's 'unconscious.'" All told, he carries the question toward the problem of conflicting mentalities:

> I believe that the most important task confronting *Beowulf* scholars—one with repercussions on the whole of Old English poetry and beyond—is to reassess how the poem's rhetorical patterning transforms "themes" into poetry.

Themes do become poetry when, as it has been argued, epochal contrast turns poetry into epistemology, into existential assertion of new worlds. "Rhetorical patterning" enters the picture when portions of older worlds—and stories—are rearranged according to new fields of meaning.

When words replace deeds, as they do early in English poetry, there ceases to be any necessary, that is, external, arrangement to narrative, since "connections" then are not spatial or structural, but associative and meaningful. The march of events melts and runs off into the stream of consciousness, which can flow, it seems, in almost any channel, if, as some would say, more rapidly downhill. Thought lives and operates in a different kind of space than does action. Pagan or Christian there is less externalized act.

Surely, one might say, a lot of good, old-fashioned action obviously survives in *Beowulf*—there are three fights after all and numerous, as it were, zero-grade actions of coming and going. But there are still many more speeches than actions. The movement is from "gold hoard to word-hoard." The "exchange of words" becomes "a central fact of life"; and "what we see, therefore, is the emergence of a hero not only as a man of action but also as a speaker" (Stevens). Actional, epic structure is working its way toward the essentially Western form of numinous speech called soliloquy. All this shows in *Beowulf*, however, because of the poem's earliness and boundary position. Great archaic icebergs have yet to melt completely in the warm seas of romance. Poets and novelists coming later in the tradition revalorize no less, perhaps, but they do so less visibly, because the arena of their activity is altogether more advancedly internalized. In *Andreas* already the antihero, the devil, is advised to have his words *eall getrahtod* (well considered) (1359b), if he would *refute* the hero. It is only a step to *Paradise Lost* where heroic action—the war in heaven—is utterly otiose, or to *Paradise Regained,* by argument. The inevitable verbalization of action, perhaps, is the proverbial "stuck" tape. But as a digressionist revalorizer of culture, the *Beowulf* poet is one of the first legislators, if not the founding father, of our world. His digressions are one of the first cultural articulations of what C. S. Lewis called [in *The Discarded Image*] "the grand movement of internalization." We can see this, because what he was digressing from is still clear in our minds. Yet we cannot help but be keenly aware, because we are still digressing, that the world he has constructed does not always conform to the contours of our own, as Kierkegaard would put it, *parentheses.*

THE EGRESSION OF HRETHEL (2426–43, 2462b–71)

The poet's "digressionist" status calls for a concrete illustration—for a true digression on a digression. All the poet's digressions do not, as it has been observed, go about redefining the world of action in quite the same way. Some, like the Sigemund story (875ff.), doubtless because of the power inherent in that legend, possess considerably more narrative independence than others and, thus, tend to enter into structural patterns of anticipation. Similar, but more strongly redefinitive, are the Heremod histories (898–915, 1709b–24a). These redefine what a good king should be, though negatively, and anticipate the man-dragon himself, as does the remainder of Hrothgar's sermon (1687–1784), even the Finnsburg story (1071ff.), insofar as it has one "king" killing another. The *Beowulf* poet, like other good ones, seldom does one thing at a time. Sometimes he actually addresses his audience much like a Victorian novelist, especially in his briefer pseudognomic utterances. But closer to the present discussion is his digression on old King Hrethel's death, which appears to contain a second digression on an old man whose son dies (2444–62a). These both illustrate how a *good* king should die and thus point directly to how Beowulf will in fact die. Here we can see the poet's transformative epistemology at work, changing the "real thing" into his thing.

The message is indisputably clear: a *good* king does not take it with him—he leaves his wealth to his heirs and heads for heaven. That this message is spoken by Beowulf himself makes it all the more powerful. In summarizing his career in this last speech before his own men (2516–18a), after telling the story of Hrethel and—or as—an old man, Beowulf stresses *all that he has survived*. He has also provided us with a paradigm for right action in the face of insurmountable problems, when survival by morally acceptable means has become impossible. One of Hrethel's sons kills the other by accident; there is nothing which the old king can do about it. Hrethel's plight is epitomized by the fact that in order to do justice by one son he must see the other swinging on the gallows. Much within this subtly compounded predicament of Hrethel as a helpless old man applies to Beowulf: not actionally, as we have seen, for Beowulf can and does act (if in paradoxical circumstances), but because his too is a *feohleas gefeoht* (fixless fight) (2441a), a no-win situation. So, Hrethel, rather than "sin," dies and leaves his possesions to his rightful sons (the poet generalizes with *eaferum* [2470a], "sons," although Hrethel now has two), as a good king should. From 2468:

He then with that sorrow,   by which this hurt overtook him,
The happy company of men gave up,   God's light chose;
To his sons he left,   as does a good man,
His lands and towns   when he from life departed.

This thematic "Christian" acceptance of earthly woes and mortality is more than Hrethel's story; it anticipates the rationale of Beowulf's actions. He too will accept his fate (2813–16)—will not struggle to cling to his treasures a little bit longer. Having won them again for his people (2794–98), he gladly dies, wishing only that he had a son (2729–32a).

This righteous death, however, contrasts markedly with what the man-dragon has done. He did not *ofgeaf* (give up) (2251b, 2469a) anything; he clings to life—of a sort—and does not die "as does a good man" (2238b–41a). Quite to the contrary, he hoards his treasures, uttering his fateful "treasure words": "The great power I now enjoy" (2247a). He takes the pagan route, like old Thorir, in the *Þorskfirðinga Saga,* who acts quite *un*like Hrethel, but very much like the man-dragon:

> Þat var sagt, eitthvert sumar, at Guðmundr, sonr hans, hafði fallit í bardaga, en þat hafði þó logit verit. Þórir brá svá við þessi tíðendi, er hann frétti, at hann hvarf á brott frá búi sinu, ok vissi engi maðr, hvat af honum vaeri orðit eða hann kom niðr, en þat hafa menn fyrir satt, at hann hafi at dreka orðit or hafði lagizt á gullkistur sínar. Helzt þat ok lengi síðan, at men sá dreka fljuga ofan um þeim megin frá Þoris stöðum, ok Gullfors er kallaðr, ok yfir fjörðinn í fjall þat, er stendr yfir baenum í Hlið.

> (It was said that one summer, that Guthmundr, his son, had fallen in battle, and that he had been buried. This news disturbed Thorir so much that, when he heard it, he departed from his house and would have nothing to do with any man who would speak with him or approach him; and men told the story that he had become a flying dragon and was lying upon his chests of gold. And it turned out before long that men saw a flying dragon over by the river at Thorir's place, which is called Gold-Falls, and over the fjord in the fells which stand above the farms in Hlith.)
>
> [Guðni J. Johnsson edition]

Thorir, in a word, becomes embittered by life and, dying, takes his treasure with him. He does not accept the loss of his son as a "Christian" should. It is significant, too, that before this happens, it is said of Thorir that "Hann gerðist illr ok ódaell viðskiptis ae því meir, er hann eldist meir (He became more and more unfriendly and stingy of his goods as he grew older)." Thorir is rather more a Heremod than a Hrethel.

Beowulf's digression upon his survival of life's troubles, thus, shows how the poet's technique works. His digressions establish the framework of *values*—not necessarily actions—in which his actional passages are to be interpreted. There are many reasons for killing a dragon, natural or otherwise. The *Beowulf* poet, however, wants his audience to know precisely why *his* hero is killing *this* particular, which is to say, emblematic *man*-dragon. He thus presents the story of Hrethel (an every-old-man), as of a man who lives and dies rightly, in epochal contrast to the man-dragon Beowulf is about to fight and who, like the pagan Thorir, took his wealth to the grave with him, refusing to share it. By means of this contrast the poet redefines pagan values. The shift to idea and theme creates an impression of crude juxtaposition, but only when these value-updating passages are mistakenly read as independent narratives, not as the storial "idioms" they have become.

In this way, as Carrigan has pointed out, such a reassessment of the poet's digressions does indeed entail "repercussions of the whole of Old English poetry and beyond," precisely because his digressions do turn "'themes' into poetry." This is another way of saying the *Beowulf* poet is already turning poetry into epistemology. Even though, as Stevens has recently argued, "few" scholars "would even admit that the notorious digressions are, in fact, 'digressions' if that word, as generally defined, is taken to mean 'an excursive passage,'" there is still no need to explain them away. There are digressions in *Beowulf*—good and powerful ones.

The present digression, however, does contain a few textual problems best handled here, before Beowulf's last speech carries us back to the fight proper. The first of these falls in lines 2435–40 and turns of the problem of *frēawine* (lord [and friend]) (2438a), which both Klaeber and Dobbie, among standard editors, see as inappropriate to Herebeald, who is not Haethcyn's lord, but his brother. The usual way out of this problem is to rationalize like Klaeber, who qualifies his doubts with "*frēawine* is not entirely inappropriate, since Herebeald is the elder brother and heir apparent"; or to emend *frēawine* to *frēowine*, (noble friend) (cf. 430a), after Bugge. Along the first line, Wrenn-Bolton cite Chambers's translation, "smote him who should have been his lord," with approbation. But none of these solutions are necessary, because the problem lies, not in the object, the meaning of which is clear, but in the verb and its narrative context. The poet's diction and meaning may be somewhat more subtle than has been assumed.

The verb *swencan*, as the causative of *swincan* (to labor, be in trouble) does not carry the concrete sense of "to shoot" or "to smite," etc., as it often has been translated. But because it has been taken for granted that all the poet's references here (2435b, 2438a, 2439b, 2440a) are only to Herebeald, including, of course, the problematic *frēawine,* the poet's expression *flāne geswencte* (vexed [troubled, distressed, etc.] with an arrow) (2438b), has been taken metaphorically and concretized into "killed (physically)": whereas its first meaning is emotional. Yet the context would indicate that *frēawine* points to Hrethel. In a word, with one and the same arrow Haethcyn killed his brother *and* brought his father to despair. We may thus translate the text as it stands:

Was for the oldest   all wrongly
By his kinsman's deeds   his deathbed spread,
After him Haethcyn   from a horn-tipped bow,
His friend and lord,   with an arrow brought to despair—
He missed his mark   and his kinsman shot (to death),
One brother, the other,   with a bloody dart.

(2435–40)

The expression, "his deathbed spread" does not mean that the arrow killed Herebeald on the spot, but only that he did die of the wound— most likely in the bed which is later sadly viewed as *windge* (windswept) (2456a). An overconfident identification of being shot with being (instantly) killed has, however, contributed to the problem of *frēawine,* through an unjustified concretization of the poet's also most likely and poignantly literal "with an arrow brought to despair." After all, Hrethel died of the wrenching love for his lost son and the staggering frustration of not being able to right such an impossible wrong. Syntax as well as narrative point to the *hyne* (him) (2437a), as Hrethel, for he is, after all, the main subject of the passage and already the referent of two telling, third person pronouns (2432a, 2433b), as well as the recipient of the title *frēawine folca* (friend and lord of the folk) (2429a). The *hyne* in question is, further, immediately diambiguized by the phrase *his frēawine* (his friend and lord) (2438a), according to an appositive pattern the poet frequently uses. And the new statement beginning "One brother, the other" (2440a), is also explanatory, clarifying (and repeating) the occasion of Hrethel's mortal despair. The "oldest," of course, means "the oldest of Hrethel's sons," so that the old king remains in the foreground, specifically in the context of his remarkable friendliness which did not forget *sibbe* (kinship) (2431b). Only a too local and "unglued" reading can take *frēawine* as Herebeald, at the expense of the emotional impact of this accidental fratricide which holds the entire passage together.

The centrality of this emotional tragedy accounts for Beowulf's otherwise surprising, if litotic, adjective *lāðra* (more hateful) (2432b). Why should Beowulf, especially in a context of loving support, use such a negative way of expressing Hrethel's fatherly concern for him? Paternal love is not ordinarily a subject of rhetorical abuse in Old English. But when we consider how indeed Haethcyn might very well have become "hateful" to his father after the unfortunate accident, then the usage and its anticipative force becomes clear: this is what Beowulf had started out to talk about. The killing of Herebeald is not just one of a series of remembrances mentioned as a part of a general history; it is the main point. This focussing upon Hrethel's death and its cause, and the narrative integrity of Beowulf's digression, reveals, as the conventional, more fragmented reading of the passage cannot, that the *gomelan ceorle* (old man) (2444b), is not a supposititious, second old man (analogous to the editorial thief), but none other than Hrethel himself. Critical habit and narrative convention have obviated the obvious question: why should Beowulf introduce another personage at this point? A misalignment of correlative *swā*'s (2444a, 2462b) has subtly provided an erroneous narrative fulcrum for contextual dislocation; but once the question is raised, it becomes apparent that Hrethel is the only old man here, and that the correlation lies between his emotions and his action.

The phrase *giong on galgan* ([go] young on the gallows) (2446a), with its play upon *giong,* and perhaps even on *gāl* (wantonness) and *gān* a second time, is not a reference to an otherwise unmentioned and mysterious criminal youth, which could only complicate the elegiac tone of Hrethrel's tragedy, nor merely a paraphrastic way of saying "die." The reference is rather to Haethcyn, whom old Hrethel is too sad (yet feudally bound) to punish. The verb *tō gebīdanne,* here (2445a) and later (2452a), carries the sense of "to endure, abide," not only, "to wait for *or* live to see, etc." Certainly the poet is expanding upon Hrethrel's dilemma, allowing it, in his use of the consuetudinal *bið* (is [always]) (2444a), to slip into another categorical "any-old-man." But Hrethel is the living exemplum here. The verbs *rīde* (2445b) and *wrece* (2446b)—echoing *unwrecen* (2443a)—are more than syntactically subjunctive. Herebeald will go unavenged—and unsung, perhaps, because it is always too hard for an old man like Hrethel to avenge one son by killing another. Such would indeed call for a *sārigne sang* (sorry song) (2447a). The *swā* in 2444a, therefore, should not be allowed to dislocate the context; its reference is immediately adverbial, and no stop should be placed after *linnan* (lose) (2443b). Nothing can be done, because *swā biđ geōmorlic* (so devastating it is) (2444a).

That a tight opposition is intended here between Haethcyn and Herebeald can also be seen in *ōđres* ([of the] other, second) (2451b), and *se ān* (that [other] one) (2453b). There is no need to take *yrfeweardas* (guardians of inheritance) (2453a), as a mistaken genitive singular, because the poet's sense here is that Hrethel does not care to abide heirs of his second son, doubtless having set his heart upon a different succession through his first son Herebeald. The Old English presents no problems, for *gebīdan* (2452a) may take, especially with a genitive pronomial, an accusative object:

> of the other he cares not
> To live to see,   inside the dwellings,
> The inheritors,   when that (first) one has.
> (2451b–53)

In fact, there cannot really be any question of merely waiting for a second heir for any aged man. Hrethel's predicament is that, although he cannot bring himself to avenge Herebeald by punishing Haethcyn, at the same time he cannot abide everyday being reminded by the living occasion of his grief that Haethcyn's, not Herebeald's, children will succeed him. (Whether or not the poet intends another irony by having Haethcyn next killed (2481–83), we cannot tell, since we do not know how much time has elapsed or whether or not there are any heirs. But the second use of *ōđer* (the other) (2481a), for Haethcyn does seem to hearken back to the earlier death of Herebeald.) In any case, Beowulf's concern is the single story of Hrethel and two of his sons.

This focus can also be seen in the sustained reference of the third person pronoun. The antecedent of *hē* (2448b) and the grammar of the subsequent *him* (2448b) are not in themselves clear. They must be determined from the narrative. There is, again, no need to introduce a second old man saving a problematically criminal son. The reference is to Hrethel though a reflexive use of *him*. And whether or not we restore *helpan* (2448b) as either an infinitive or a weak feminine noun, we may translate:

> and he cannot help himself,
> Old and helpless with age,   cannot do anything.
> (2448b–49)

This reflexive reading of *him,* furthermore, anticipates the poet's repetition of the same idea at the conclusion of this digression on Hrethel and, thus, serves to unify the entire passage. The equally tight rhetorical function and reference of the second *swā* (2462b) comes, thus, to light. Again we may translate directly:

> not at all might he
> Upon the killer   the feud make good;
> Nor none the sooner he that battle-ruler   might hate
> For his hateful deeds,   though to him dear he was not.
> (2464b–67)

Hrethel ought, but cannot hang Haethcyn, who more than a mere warrior rules already the family's fate. And again we can see in the phrase *lāðum dǣdum* (for his hateful deeds) (2467a), the reason why Beowulf began by saying he was not *lāðra* (more hateful) (2432a) to Hrethel than his other sons. The second *lāðum* concludes what the first *lāðra* introduces. It is a story of *sorhge* (sorrow) (2468a); and the gender of *sorhge* resolves the difficulties of 2468b: after the instrumental *þē, sīo* does not modify *sār,* but supplants it as a pronominal subject, so that we may translate literally, "by which with respect to him this (sorrow) to great hurt led," or more idiomatically:

> He then with that sorrow   by which this hurt overtook him,
> The happy company of men gave up,   God's light chose.
> (2468–69)

All this, of course, old Hrethel does in distinct contrast to Beowulf's immediate enemy, the man-dragon, let alone a character like the outright pagan Thorir. The man-dragon does not give up the company of men voluntarily (2223–24, 2407–11, 3064b–65), nor does he surrender his property to his heirs (2247ff.), let alone choose God's light, "as does a good man . . . when he from life departed" (2470–71). But it is old Hrethel who does all this.

Heeding in this way the tragic mode of Beowulf's digression reveals the general working of the poet's technique. In this case he inserts a genuinely lyrical passage within his larger narrative. The complexity of the result has recently been illustrated, for example, by an argument that *rīdend,* in the phrase *rīdend swefað* (riders sleep) (2457b), should be translated as "ridings sleep," in conjunction with *rēote* (2457a) taken as naming a musical instrument, the *rota.* Although this attractive suggestion is subtly at odds with the subsequent turn to the want of the sound of harps

(2458b), insofar as it is unlikely that the poet would introduce into a categorical passage a particular distinction between two kinds of instruments, nevertheless it still points to the richness of the poet's diction. For the word *rīdend* as "riders" (2457b), in the context of loving care and children, e.g., *yrfeweardas* as "heirs" (2453a), along with a series of words like *būre* (bower) (2455b), *reste* (bed, bedding) (2456b), and *hoðman* (dark, darkness, grave) (2458a), suggests a conscious overlay of love and death and the bed and the grave, worthy of Marvell's "fine and private place" (cf. the poet's use of *leger*, 3043a, and *legerbedde*, 1007b, with *swefeð*, 1008a). The son's *būre* (bower) is not likely to be a *wīnsele* (joyous wine-hall) (2456a), but its intimate emptiness, like the whole world now, seems to the sad father *eall tō rūm* (everything all too roomy!) (2461b). The bower recalls the hall, which now will never be filled with the cherished heirs. We may thus translate:

> He sees grievously sad   in his son's bower
> A (happy) winehall deserted,   windswept bedding
> Of joy bereft—   riders sleep,
> Those warriors in the dark;   nor is there any sound of the harp,
> (Nor) games in the (court)yards,   as there once were.
>
> (2455–59)

Although an immediately musical reading, therefore, of 2457 seems unlikely, still it remains a latent possibility and reminds us of how the entire passage resonates with the sad echoes of the *gumdrēam* (the [happy] company of men) (2469a), now utterly shattered for aged Hrethel. This "life," emblematically considered as the problem of human life and death, keeps the human predicament, and the profound alternatives the poet is considering, starkly before us and readies us for the remainder of what Beowulf has to say, whose voice now acquires a depth and a resonance of centuries of old Hrethels. An empty room and windswept bedding "are all that is left where once were the stir and bustle of human life, and 'fate, free will, foreknowledge absolute,' in some form and dialect or other were by turns discussed," as Thoreau puts it later—after Milton.

What is left to say, of course, is how Haethcyn died and how, by implication, Beowulf got to be king. The history of how Beowulf conducted himself as the three brothers fell one by one to fate (cf. his statement 2813–16) carries the past into the narrative present, as this moves forward into the fight with the man-dragon. The structural and thematic centrality of Beowulf's final "boast" complements his enemy's "lament" and calls for its own discussion and an end to digression. It remains but to say that the modal revalorizing aspect of digression probably indicates *lateness,* not because it necessarily involves a more run-on style and fewer discrete, self-contained verses, or even that it occurs more frequently, but because it reveals a doubleness of vision, an interpretation of action, rather than action itself. R. W. McTurk has concluded that at least as far as the poetic edda are concerned "variation does not differ sufficiently between the groups (early and late) to show a chronological development." But the eddic poetry compared to Old English is all relatively late, and the general brevity of verse forms precludes any genuinely useful comparison to Old English poetry, in which, so to speak, there is room for extended variation of a digressive nature. The central fact of all digressions, phrasal or storial, is that they imply a poetic stance outside of the action or objects they treat. And Beowulf and old Hrethel about whom Beowulf speaks are decidedly outside of Heremod's tradition. They seem more in the Christian camp, as the homiletic collocation of the inability of one man to help another might indicate. For when a man dies:

> ne maeg nan oðres gehelpan. Ac hi þonne
> onginnað singan swiðe sorhfulne sang.

> [nor can anyone help another. But they then
> sing a terribly sorrowful song.]
> (*Vercelli Homily* 9, Paul E. Szarmach edition)

Apposed Word Meanings
and Religious Perspectives

Fred C. Robinson

In his magisterial edition of *Beowulf,* Frederick Klaeber refers almost despairingly to "the problem of finding a formula which satisfactorily explains the peculiar spiritual atmosphere of the poem." At times Klaeber thought that the poet sought to "modernize" the pagan society of sixth-century Scandinavia by depicting it as Christian but that his modernization is marred by lapses into historical accuracy, as when the Danes are shown worshiping idols. At other times, he thought, perhaps we are to assume that some of the Danes at Heorot were Christians and that they reverted to paganism under the stress of Grendel's attacks. Tolkien insists that the poem is clearly set in pagan Scandinavia and yet sees Hrothgar as a kind of Christian monotheist moving among pagan compatriots. Brodeur too thinks the setting is pagan, but the Christian poet, he feels, would have found it unthinkable that such noble pagans could be damned, and therefore he depicts them as acknowledging the Christian God. Other readers have appealed to allegory or to the naive ahistoricism of the Middle Ages to account for the fact that, although the poem is set in pagan Scandinavia and the poet describes and condemns the pagan rites of the Danes (ll. 175–88), the legendary characters often speak with a piety that makes them sound like Christians.

The least persuasive explanations of the problem are those which proceed from an assumption that the poet was vague or absent-minded in his characterization of the religious state of his legendary figures. A Christian Anglo-Saxon, whether in the age of Bede or the age of Ælfric,

From Beowulf *and the Appositive Style.* © 1985 by the University of Tennessee Press. Translations supplied by the editor.

was not casual or vague-minded about whether a person was Christian or heathen. And the *Beowulf* poet carefully reminds us throughout his poem that the events he is narrating took place in another age and another world. His firm historical sense also rules out Klaeber's suggestion that the poet intends us to think (but neglects to tell us) that there were both Christians and pagans living together in the northern lands of the heroic age. Both the poet and his audience knew well that sixth-century Scandinavians were heathens. And lest it be thought that Anglo-Saxons tended to forget the heathenism of the Scandinavians as time wore on, we should recall that, in the *Chronicle,* charters, poems, and saints' lives, Old English *hæðen* (as well as Latin *paganus*) was virtually a synonym for *Dene* (i.e., "Scandinavian"). Indeed, the association between heathenism and Scandinavians became ever stronger in Anglo-Saxon England as the centuries passed. The vaguely pious heroes of *Beowulf,* then, would not have been mistaken for Christians by an Anglo-Saxon audience.

The obliqueness with which the poet presents his characters' spiritual status, averring that they are pagans and yet presenting them in a way that keeps their paganism in abeyance, is closely consonant with the studied laconism and indirection of the appositive style. It is through this style, I believe, that the poet creates a spiritual setting in which his audience can assess the men of old for what they were. He does not deny his characters' heathenism but uses the traditional diction and appositional effects to free the audience of the mind-numbing alarm which a graphic depiction of a pagan society would cause. He frees them, that is, to reflect, to assess, to sympathize, and even to admire. The mechanism by which he achieves this liberation of judgment is the subject of the present chapter, which will argue that the Cædmonian renovation of Old English poetic diction had left the *Beowulf* poet with a vocabulary in which many words had double meanings—pre-Cædmonian and post-Cædmonian—and that the poet systematically exploited these double meanings to create that "peculiar spiritual atmosphere" remarked by Klaeber. To describe the semantic layering of the Christianized poetic diction of Old English I have indulged in a metaphoric extension of my term "appositive." The term is meant to suggest an analogy between a syntax and narrative structure wherein elements are paratactically (and often ambiguously) juxtaposed and words which carry two "apposed" meanings. In both kinds of apposition, two elements are found together, with no expressed logical connection; just as we must refer to context to construe the syntax and relevance of appositive compounds and unpunctuated clauses, so too we must refer to context to determine how the apposed word meanings are to be understood.

The ambiguous poetic words appear to hold in suspension two apposed word meanings because of the double perspective which the poet maintains throughout *Beowulf*. As the poet's distinctive voice interchanges with the voices of his characters, we strongly sense that we are experiencing the narrative simultaneously from the point of view of the pre-Christian characters and from the point of view of the Christian poet, and either of two senses of ambiguous words seems to be operative, depending on which perspective we adopt. Before examining this ambiguous vocabulary and its bearing on the poem's spiritual atmosphere, it will be necessary to consider the double perspective and how it works in the poem.

In reading *Beowulf* it is important to notice that the monsters are presented from two points of view. To the pagan characters in the poem, these creatures are *eotenas* [giants], *fifelcynn* [monster race], *scinnan* [phantoms], *scynscaþan* [demonic foes], *scuccan* [evil spirits], and *ylfe* [goblins]— all terms from pagan Germanic demonology, which the characters (and the poet when he is adopting the characters' perspective) use to refer to the monsters. But the poet in his own voice tells his audience much more about these preternatural creatures, including the true genealogy of the Grendelkin: they are monstrous descendants of Cain, whose progeny was banished by God and punished with the Flood. They are the *gigantas* of the Vulgate, who remain in conflict with the Lord of Heaven. Hrothgar knows nothing of this background (1355–57). Also, the poet, but not the Danes or Geatas, knows that Grendel is God's adversary (786, 1682), a servant of hell (788, 1274), of the Devil's company (756), and feuding with God (711, 811). His term *orcneas*, a hybrid composed of a Latin word for "infernal demon" and a Germanic word for the walking dead, epitomizes the dual perception of the monsters. And this dual perception is of signal importance to our understanding of the poem. When Beowulf, impelled by his heathen ideals of conduct, pits his strength against what he calls a *þyrs* [giant] (426), he is unwittingly allying himself with the true God of Christianity in His eternal opposition to diabolic forces of evil. This lends dignity to the heathen hero, who, without knowing it, is fighting on the right side after all.

The poet maintains a dual perception of the monsters by characterizing them in terms which will have meaning in both the Christian and pagan context. The eerie light that "of eagum stod / ligge gelicost [shone forth from his eyes / most like flame]" (726–27) may seem at first to mark Grendel as purely an ogre of Germanic legend, such as the *haugbúi* and other gleaming-eyed monsters of Icelandic saga, but the English life of St. Margaret tells us that when the Devil in dragon's form assaults the saint "of his toþan leome ofstod, . . . and of his eagan swilces fyres lyg [from his teeth shone a gleam, . . . and from his eyes a flame of such fire]." The mere where the Grendelkin dwell seems compact of details from folklore horror tales, and yet we know that it also has unmistakable features drawn from the description of hell in the *Visio Pauli,* which the Blickling Homilist also used. This studied conflation of the demons from Germanic mythology with demons from Christian culture was aided no doubt by the efforts of other Anglo-Saxons to make sense of the parallel demonologies of pagans and Christians. King Alfred in his Boethius translation associates the Titans of pagan Classical mythology with Nimrod and the giants of the Old Testament, while homilists and translators of the Bible sometimes adapted the old Germanic terms for monsters to biblical phenomena. To the characters in the poem *Beowulf,* the monsters have meaning only in terms of the pagan's dark mythology of evil; to the Christian Anglo-Saxons attending the poem this meaning is equally apparent, but they see other meanings as well, because they understand the true nature of evil and its connections with Cain and the Devil. So carefully does the poet maintain this two-leveled portrayal of the monsters that in the last part of the poem he need only introduce a monster with well-established credentials in both worlds—a dragon—and trust that the audience will, without further prompting, see the creature in its full complexity. It is on one level of perception like the dragon that Sigemund slew; on another it has those connotations of Satanic evil with which Bible and commentary had long invested it.

The same double perspective is maintained, I believe, in the characterization of the heroes in the poem. Their thoughts and their language are circumscribed by the pagan world in which they live, and when at times their speeches seem to have a Christian resonance, the audience is supposed to recognize that these are but coincidences of similar elements in two alien cultures, coincidences which inevitably give dignity to the old heroes as viewed by Christian eyes but which betray no Christian revelation in heathen minds. A prime example is the speech which is often tendentiously called "Hrothgar's sermon" (1700–84). Because Hrothgar advises Beowulf against overweening pride, avarice, and irascible violence, some scholars have wanted to see this as a Christian homily on the Seven Deadly Sins, and many parallels in Scripture and commentary have been adduced. But there is nothing in the speech that is not equally accordant with Germanic pre-Christian piety, and there are some things that are appropriate to only such a context. For it is a speech about Germanic leadership, about fame, about the gifts of men, about fulfilling one's destined role in heroic society, about sudden changes of fortune (*edwenden*), and, above all, about how a warrior leader must always purchase the loyalty of his followers with generous gifts. Since people cannot be generous if they are avaricious and cannot monitor their own behavior if they are consumed with arrogance, Hrothgar inevitably warns against vices which Christians also deplore. But this warning bespeaks no Christian illumination mysteriously vouchsafed to a pagan Germanic king. Rather, it reveals a kind of natural, universal wisdom that any noble heathen might share with a Christian. The *Beowulf* poet no doubt emphasized these points where Christian and pagan morality converged in Hrothgar's speech in the hope that the audience would notice them and would marvel that this sixth-century king, though deprived of revelation, could, in his wisdom, strike so close to Christian truths. His doing so would give him dignity and stature in the listeners' estimation, but it would not mislead them into supposing he was a Christian. They would be regretfully aware that he was musing on matters which were ultimately beyond his understanding, since he lacks the theological framework and vocabulary necessary for dealing with them definitively, and, like other pagans, he stands beyond the reach of Christ's redemption. This poignant limitation in Hrothgar's views on moral conduct should be all the clearer to the poem's audience because of the telling description of the king's demeanor as he begins his speech. The poet shows Hrothgar gazing long at the sword hilt with the biblical account of the Deluge engraved upon it. Poet and audience know exactly what the flood that slew the giant race was and whence it came, but Hrothgar does not. Since he has no biblical knowledge, his gaze is a blind gaze. He is in a way like Aeneas gazing at the shield which a god had fashioned for him. The events depicted on the shield are from the future, and Aeneas cannot construe them, but Virgil and his audience could. As with Aeneas, so with Hrothgar, we admire all the more the partial understanding he achieved, since we know that he, unlike us, did not share knowledge with a higher power: "miratur rerumque ignarus imagine gaudet [he marvels and rejoices at all these images, though he does not know what they mean]" (8, 730).

But this reading of Hrothgar's speech, it may be said, takes no notice of the pious tone of his references to the Deity. Would not his allusions to *Waldend* [ruler], *Metod* [creator], and *mihtig God* [mighty God] mark his disquisition unambiguously as the utterance of a Christian? This question brings us back to the matter of the polysemous vocabulary which resulted from the Christianization of Old English poetic diction by Cædmon and his successors. We may begin with the terms for God which this reformed heroic diction offered the *Beowulf* poet, or at least those terms which he selected for his legendary characters to utter when they referred to a higher being. Usually scholars take the scop's allusion to *se Ælmihtiga* in line 92 as the first time in the poem when a character mentions the Christian God. Actually, it is not the scop who speaks the words *se Æmihtiga* but the poet, who is presenting the song of creation in indirect discourse: "*cwæð þæt se Ælmihtiga eorðan worhte.*" It is reasonable, however, to assume that the poet may have intended us to think that this is the actual term used by the scop for the Creator. But there is no authority whatever for the capital letter *Æ-* which forces modern readers to assume that this allusion refers unambiguously to the Christian Deity. Anglo-Saxon scribes did not capitalize the first letter of *nomina sacra* or of any proper names. Ignoring the modern editors' capitalization in *ælmihtiga,* we are free to translate line 92, "He said that the all-powerful one created the earth." Who would the "all-powerful one" be? If the speaker is a heathen, as we should expect the scop in Heorot to be, then *se ælmihtiga* would refer to one of the pagan gods: compare *hinn almáttki áss* in the heathen oath of the Icelanders referring to Thor. Or, if the scop should be not specifically pagan but rather a pre-Christian man of no very specific religious beliefs (somewhat like the nameless atheling who recounts the sparrow simile in Bede's account of the conversion of Edwin), then *se ælmihtiga* might refer to "the all-powerful being (whoever he might be)." Old English *ælmihtig* and its cognates in other Germanic languages obviously did not mean "the Christian God" before contact with Christians, who, upon converting any Germanic nation, usually appropriated the word as a term for God the Father (probably because of its similarity in sense to the Christian Latin *omnipotens*). Such adaptation of pre-Christian vocabulary to Christian concepts was a momentous event in the history of each of the Germanic dialects. Christine Fell has recently pointed out how similar was the development of a Christian terminology for the Deity from pagan diction in Old Icelandic and in Old English: "Snorri, presenting a scholarly critique of poetry, discusses the proper poetic appellations for Christ alongside the proper appellations for heathen gods and earthly kings, and makes it easy for us to see how traditional pre-Christian phrasing and vocabulary could be consciously adapted. When, for example, he points out the ambivalence of a phrase such as 'king of men' or 'king of Jerusalem' which might be used of Christ or a secular king, he is exposing and analysing the process of thought which underlies Cædmon's *moncynnes weard* [mankind's lord]." [In *Hagiography and Medieval Literature: A Symposium,* edited by Hans Bekker-Nielsen, et al.] In both languages (and presumably in all Germanic languages) the Christianization of the vocabulary was a matter not of the displacement of pre-Christian meanings by Christian meanings but rather of the extension of pre-Christian meanings to include Christian concepts, and so the words retain at least vestiges of early meanings while assuming new Christian senses. Once we remove the capital letter from *ælmihtiga* in *Beowulf* 92, it becomes clear that the word is a polysemous term equally appropriate in pagan and Christian contexts and not, as Hoops and others have assumed, a term specifying the Christian Deity.

Considering the true semantic range of *ælmihtig,* I have said, the heathen scop in Heorot could be referring in line 92 either to a specific Germanic god or to simply "whatever omnipotent one created the earth." The *Beowulf* poet would not be the only Germanic Christian who thought his ancestors may have been capable of sensing the existence of a Creator and of directing their piety toward this dimly perceived Creator rather than toward Germanic gods such as Woden, Thunor, and Tiw. In Icelandic sagas there are several pagan characters who, disregarding the Germanic gods, refer to "the unknown creator" of the world and men, seeming to intuit from their observation of the ordered universe that some supreme being must have been its author. Since the intuitive process of these characters is analogous with the scop's intuition in his hymn to the creator, it may be useful to recall one or two of them here. Arnorr kerlingarnef in the *Flateyjarbók,* for example, suspects that the true God is "he who created the sun to give light and warmth to this earth," and Thorsteinn in *Vatnsdœla saga* speaks of "him who created the sun and the whole world, whoever he may be." Both Arnorr and Thorsteinn are presented as pagan characters moving in a pagan world. The same theme of the exceptionally perceptive pagan who can sense through a kind of instinct or natural goodness the true God behind distortions of paganism can be found among Anglo-Saxon writers. We have already seen that St. Boniface thought that the pagan Saxons and Wends observed the essence of the law and ordinances of God through some mysterious sensing of the truth, and the same is true of the Old English translation of *Orosius.* There, in a considerably elaborated version of the Latin original, the translator says that Caesar Augustus refused to accept credit for the peace that blessed his reign, since only a divine power and not any *eorðlices monnes* [earthly man's] deed could have achieved the peace. Earlier in the Old English *Orosius,* Hannibal is described by the translator as understanding, through the agency of a providential rainfall which prevented a battle, that a supreme God was at work. In both of these instances the pagan heroes' sensing of the existence of the true God is an elaboration by the Old English translator of a much vaguer statement by Orosius. Evidently this ennobling view of pre-Christian people of good will was a common one among early Germanic Christians, being shared by the sagamen, St. Boniface, the *Orosius* translator, and, I would suggest, the *Beowulf* poet. The view would have been fostered by Boethius's *Consolation of Philosophy,* and an Anglo-Saxon who knew the *Aeneid* might have fancied that Aeneas's allusion to "the all-seeing mind that knows the right" confirmed the existence of prescient pagans.

Whether the *Beowulf* poet's audience would have taken *se ælmihtiga* as referring to a dim perception of the true God by a pious pagan or as a specific reference to one of the Germanic gods cannot be determined with certainty, and, indeed, the poet may be deliberately leaving the question open, a practice which is characteristic of his appositive strategy. The ensuing passage about the Danes sacrificing to heathen gods (175–83) would incline us toward the assumption that *se ælmihtiga* would mean to the scop the same thing that *hinn almáttki áss* meant to Icelanders in their heathen oath—that is, Thor or one of the other gods. But the fact that the word occurs in a hymn to creation could incline us toward the view that the scop is a noble heathen sensing the presence of a supreme being by observing the ordered workings of the natural world but without any real knowledge of Christianity. The only interpretation of *se ælmihtiga* that would be logically impossible is the one most commonly held by modern students and scholars of the poem, who assume from editors' capitalization of *Ælmihtiga* that this is an unambiguous reference to the Christian Deity and therefore evidence that the scop in Heorot is a Christian. *Beowulf* takes place in a heathen realm in a heathen age, and the scop's creation hymn is one that any pious heathen might sing. The assumption that now and again the heathen characters turn Christian and address themselves to the Christian Deity makes a muddle of the poet's artful strategy of using inherent ambiguities in the Christianized Old English vocabulary to present the men of old favorably and yet honestly to a Christian Anglo-Saxon audience.

The fact that the ambiguity of the vocabulary provides a meaning appropriate to the poem's pagan setting does not mean that the Christian sense of the words is inoperative. *Se ælmihtiga* in line 92 is actually spoken by the *Beowulf* poet, who is reporting the scop's creation hymn in indirect discourse. To the Christian poet the words would necessarily have suggested the specifically Christian meaning as well as the more general pre-Christian sense, which is the only one appropriate for his character, the scop. The poet and his audience lived after that renovation of the Old English poetic language initiated by Cædmon, and for them terms like *ælmihtiga, alwealde* [all-wielder], *frea* [lord], *metod* [creator], and *sigora waldend* [ruler of victories] inevitably suggested the Christian God. But in *Beowulf* the poet is returning that traditional diction of Old English poetry to a pre-Cædmonian, pre-Christian setting where it could have none of the Cædmonian meanings. Therefore, each time the poet's audience heard a character in the poem utter a Christianized Germanic word for a higher being, they would necessarily have had two apposed meanings in mind: the pre-Christian meaning, which was the only one the pagan characters could know, and the postconversion meaning which had become dominant by the time of the poet.

When we imagine the poet's audience sorting through the dual meanings of words and allocating to each the sense appropriate to its context, the process seems at first rather complicated, but in fact it is the same process that goes on throughout the poem as the audience hears nouns describing lord or leader and decides whether an earthly lord or the heavenly lord is meant. *Dryhten* occurs twenty-nine times in *Beowulf,* fifteen times referring to one of the characters in the poem and fourteen times referring to a higher being. But no one would find it complicated to determine whether earthly or heavenly lord is the meaning. When Wiglaf "dryhtne sinne driorigne fand [found his lord bleeding]," it can only be his dying king; when the poet says it is well for one "æfter deaðdæge drihten secean [to seek the Lord after his deathday]," we know he means God. Sometimes Old English poets used the dual meanings of *dryhten* with deliberate punning effect, a notable example being *The Seafarer* 41–43.

It is plausible, then, to assume that the poet's audience had the limberness of mind to differentiate between those contexts which presuppose a pre-Christian meaning for a term for a higher being and those which presuppose a postconversion meaning. When the poet in his own voice refers to *waldendes hyldo* (2292–93), we know he means "the grace of God," for a Christian knows of such Christian doctrines. But *waldend* in other contexts can mean quite different things. In the *Chronicle* poems it refers to English kings, and it can also mean simply "owner" or "master," as in *The Wanderer* 78 and in *Boethius* ("Ælc mon biþ wealdend ðæs

ðe he welt [each man is the master of that which he owns]"). *Waldend*
also refers to pagan gods, as when the Old English translator of Orosius,
in an expansion of his Latin original, describes the deification of Liber:
"hi hine æfter hys dæge heom for god hæfdon and hy eft sædon þæt he
wære ealles gewinnes wealdend [after his day they had him for a god,
and they said that he was the lord of all war]." We must bear this full
range of meanings for *wealdend* in mind when we read Wiglaf's statement
that the dead Beowulf must abide in the keeping of *wealdend*: "he longe
sceal / on ðæs waldendes wære geþolian" (3108–9). The poet and his
audience know that Wiglaf lived before Old English *waldend* had acquired
the meaning "Christian God." Would they not then have assumed that
for Wiglaf it would have meant something other than what it had come
to mean for them? In the sentence just quoted from *Orosius* we also see
the word *god* used in a way requiring discrimination of meanings. Since
the use of a definite or indefinite article with common nouns is not
compulsory in Old English, and since Anglo-Saxon scribes had no convention of capitalizing the first letter of nomina sacra, the words "hi hine
. . . for god hæfdon" could be translated either "they had him for a god"
or "they had him for God." Context indicates that the former meaning
is correct here, since we know that the pagans being spoken of here
believed in many gods and did not therefore take Liber Pater for the one
supreme God. In other sentences, however, the ambiguity is irresolvable.
In the Old English *Orosius*, book 6, chapter 9, for example, we are told
that Domitian "bead þæt mon on gelice to him onbugan scolde swa to
gode." Does this mean "he commanded that people should bow down
to him as to God" or "he commanded that people should bow down to
him as to a god"? Bately [in her edition] capitalizes the *g* of *gode*, indi-
cating that she assumes the first interpretation, but in the earlier edition
by Joseph Bosworth the *g* is uncapitalized, and Bosworth translates "they
had him for a god." Reference to the Latin original—"dominus sese ac
deum uocari scribi colique iusserit"—tells us nothing, for Latin, like Old
English, does not require articles before common nouns. Old English
terms for the deity like *god*, then, were simply ambiguous. In most cases
context removed the ambiguity, but in passages where both pagan and
Christian gods are in question, as in the *Orosius* passage just cited or in
treatises like the Old English Boethius, where the nature of the god being
discussed is itself somewhat problematic, the ambiguities of the word are
real and obvious. In the Cotton Otho A. vi manuscript of *The Consolation
of Philosophy*, for example, we find the Old English scribe himself puzzling
over whether *god* represents the name of the Christian Deity or the com-

mon noun *gōd* "the good." He often tries to make a distinction by marking the vowel of *gōd* long or by doubling the vowel, but as Sedgefield notes in the glossary of his edition, "the two are occasionally confused, *God* being written *good* or *gód*."

The ambiguity of words like *ælmihtig, alwalda, dryhten, god,* and *metod,* which have a pre-Cædmonian meaning coexisting with a postconversion Christian meaning, was, I believe, seized upon by the *Beowulf* poet and was artfully exploited in a way that is characteristic of his style of appositional reticence in telling the tale of Beowulf. By restricting his names for the higher being(s) to words which have two possible referents, Christian and pre-Christian, and then placing these words in a poem in which simultaneous Christian and pre-Christian contexts are pervasively present, he has solved in a way that is seriously meaningful the problem that is central to his theme of cultural reconciliation, the problem of what to call the supernatural forces to which the characters in the poem appeal. To give them Christian names like *Christ, Hælend* [Savior], *Nergend* [Savior], or *Halig Gæst* [Holy Ghost] would be patently absurd. To revive the Germanic pantheon and speak of *Woden, Tiw,* and *Thunor* would shock a Christian audience and would invite censorship from Christian copyists. More seriously, it would alienate the poet's audience from the very world to which it is his purpose to reconcile them. He solves the dilemma by exploiting the ambiguities of a poetic diction which had been semantically stratified by the Cædmonian renovation. A further example will help clarify some of the details of his strategy.

When Beowulf and his Geatisc companions complete their voyage to Denmark, we are told, "Gode þancedon / þæs þe him yþlade eaðe wurdon" (227–28). And the modern editors' invariable practice of capitalizing the first letter of *Gode* creates the problem so often remarked by critics: how could pagan Geatas pray to the Christian God? But when we return to the original, uncapitalized form of the manuscript, we can translate the sentence, "They gave thanks to a god for the fact that the ocean journey had been an easy one." That is the meaning of the sentence in the context of the pagan world inhabited by the characters in the poem. But another context is simultaneously present: the shared world of poet and audience, which is the Christian world. Speaking, as it were, over the heads of his pagan characters, the poet often addresses specifically Christian comments to his Christian contemporaries, remarking sadly that the spiritual ignorance of the men of old will cost them an eternity in hell (183–88), explaining the biblical origins of Grendel (104–14, 1258–67), alluding to the Old Testament account of the Deluge with a cryptic brevity which bespeaks confidence of shared information (114, 1689–91), and reiterating regularly that God ruled the world in the days of the men of old (who were ignorant of Him) just as He rules it now. In this Christian context embracing poet and audience, any occurrence of *god* (or of *metod, alwalda,* or *frea,* etc.) will inevitably suggest the Christian meaning. So, when the poet says that Beowulf and his men *gode þancedon,* the Christian audience knows that on the level of the characters in the poem, with their limited perception and their pre-Cædmonian diction, the noun could only refer to whatever god they knew—Thunor or Woden or perhaps "him who created the sun and the whole world, whoever he may be." But on the level of the poet and his audience, it is commonly known who the supreme being really was at the time when the Geatas were addressing their thanks to whatever god they perceived. Perhaps poet and audience felt about the heathen gods as St. Boniface and his fellow missionaries are said to have felt when they confronted, with sorrow and compassion, the heathen Saxons worshiping their deities: "The heathen gods were, after all, dim adumbrations of the one Divine Being, 'ignorantly worshipped.'" The pervasive homonymy in Anglo-Saxon words for a higher being was ideally suited to a poet who wished to affirm the distance between Christian contemporaries and noble pagan ancestors while simultaneously poeticizing a kind of cultural-linguistic fellowship between the two. It is this homonymy which enables the poet to achieve his complex and moving tone of mingled admiration and regret.

Despite the stern anathemas of an Alcuin or an Augustine, there were men of comprehensive sympathies who, though not blinking at the inevitable destiny of pagans, did strain to envision them with compassion. We see this in Minucius Felix's observation that "those who would see Jupiter as the all-ruler are mistaken in the name, yet they agree there is a single highest power," and we see it in the Second Vatican Mythographer's suggestion that a single god is the reality underlying Sol, Apollo, Diana, and the other divine names of the pagans; and, most important, we can, according to one recent study, see it on Germanic soil in Snorri's prologue to the *Prose Edda.* Evidently the early Christian view that pagan gods were simply disguises of the devil coexisted with conceptions of the pagan gods as imperfect realizations of the true Deity or as mistaken names for what would later be identified as God. Amid such various conceptions of the nature of pagan gods, it is not surprising that the *Beowulf* poet should discern in the historically based ambiguities of Old English poetic diction a strategy for representing in a complex and sympathetic way the pagans' theological gropings.

At a later stage in the Middle Ages, Dante faced an analogous problem in his portrayal of the good pagan Virgil. Introducing himself as one who lived "in the time of the false and lying gods (nel tempo de li dei falsi e bugiardi)" (*Inferno* 1, 72), Virgil refers to the Christian God in the only terminology he knows. Christ harrowing hell is simply "a mighty one (un possente)" (*Inferno* 4, 53), and God the Father is "that Emperor who reigns above" (quello Imperador che lassu regna)" (*Inferno* 1, 124). Dante and his audience could admire the great poet as he makes his respectful, vague references to God, while at the same time they would feel the poignancy of his limited vision of that God. (Another device used by both Dante and the Beowulf poet is the unwitting scriptural allusion: Hrothgar [942–46] and Virgil [*Inferno* 8, 45] both echo Luke 11:27 but in pathetic ignorance that they are doing so.) With Dante, as with the *Beowulf* poet, the aim is for noble pagans to use terms for the higher being which are historically appropriate to the speaker but at the same time close enough to the Christian religious vocabulary to soften the focus on pagan piety. A partial analogy in the modern world would be a novel written by an English-speaking Christian about pious Moslems. If the novelist's purpose were to distance his Moslem characters from his Christian audience and to emphasize their exotic infidelism, he might portray them calling on Allah or Mohammed, ritually facing Mecca, and practicing polygamy. If his purpose on the other hand were to induce his readers to sympathize with the Moslems in the narrative, he might avoid detailing the more exotic rites of Islam and translate *Allah* into "God." Such a translation would not misrepresent the religious condition of the Moslems, for the audience would know that their religion is not that of the Christians, and they would know that the Arabic word for God and the Moslem conception of God differ from the Christian. But the polysemy of the word *god* would accommodate both the Christian and the Moslem conceptions without confusing the two. In *Beowulf* a poet is working in a somewhat similar way to accommodate the pagan forebears to the Christian world view of the Anglo-Saxons.

The *Beowulf* poet's pervasive play on the dual meanings of names for a higher being in the poem is possible, of course, only because he has selected with such meticulous care the terms that his characters use in their references to the deity they address. Specifically Christian terms for Christ, the Holy Ghost, and the Trinity (which are ubiquitous in the poetry of Cynewulf, the anonymous religious poets, and the various Christian narratives) are scrupulously avoided by the *Beowulf* poet. The popular system of God terms consisting of a base word combined with the genitive *engla* [of angels] (*engla cyning* [king of angels], *helm engla* [protector of angels], *heofonengla cyning*[king of the angels of heaven], and so forth) are never used by the characters in *Beowulf,* who refer instead to *ylda waldend* [ruler of men] (1661), *sigora waldend* [ruler of victories] (2875). An even more popular expression for the Christian Deity is the system of two-part terms meaning "God's Son," such as *godes bearn* [god's child], *godes gastsunu* [god's spiritual son], and *sunu dryhtnes* [the son of the Lord]. Referring too specifically to the second person of the Trinity, these are also avoided completely by the *Beowulf* poet. The terms *nergend* and *hælend,* which occur more than 150 times in poetry outside *Beowulf* (including even some Old Testament poetry) are never used by characters in *Beowulf,* apparently because they are too specifically associated with the Savior Christ. *Milde,* which Keiser notes is an especially frequent epithet of the Christian Deity, is never used of a deity in *Beowulf.* Just as he never alludes to the Incarnation, Crucifixion, Eucharist, Redemption, Cross, church, saints, New Testament, and other cardinal elements of Christianity, the poet avoids with remarkable consistency any God terms which are specifically or exclusively Christian in their denotation, preferring instead the more equivocal terms such as *alwalda, fæder alwealda, frea ealles,* and *metod.*

Having created this artfully ambiguous terminology for his pagan characters to use, the poet himself often echoes their vague terminology in his own references to God, thus reducing the verbal impact of his theological alienation from the men of old. His purpose being to reconcile Christian Anglo-Saxons poetically to their pious but pagan forebears, he adopts the God terms of his pre-Christian characters when he refers to God himself, giving an illusion of superficial respectability to his characters, but an illusion which is poignantly transparent.

But the poet's terminology for the deity is not wholly undifferentiated from that of his heathen characters. The Christian God whom the poet and audience worship is not the same as the gods of the Germanic pantheon or as the heathens' vague premonitions of God, and the poet must make this clear. He does so repeatedly, but, except for the anguished contrasting of pagan with Christian deity in 175–88, his distinctions between the two are made in a subdued tone which does not disrupt the superficial harmony between the piety of his own day and that of the men of old. Typically the distinction is drawn in passages where heathen (or diabolic) power is operative, and the poet is concerned to emphasize that although the forces of evil enjoyed supernatural powers (as medieval

Christianity readily acknowledged), this must not confuse us as to who the real God is.

When the blood of Grendel melts the blade of the giant sword in 1605–8, the poet says that it was a notable marvel or miracle ("þæt wæs wundra sum") (1607). But he then hastens to contrast this miracle of the diabolic forces with the much greater miracle of the true God, who controls the times and seasons of the world: "Þæt is soð metod [that is the true ordainer of fate]" (1611). Similarly, when he describes the preternaturally powerful curse laid on the gold of the dragon's hoard by a heathen charm (3051–52), he adds that its power can be overturned at any time by the greater power of "god sylfe, sigora soðcyning [god himself, true king of victories]" (3054–55). Only the poet in his own voice uses the modifiers soð and self with terms for God, for these are the words which Old English writers habitually use to differentiate the true God of Christianity from the false gods of the heathen. Thus in Cynewulf's *Juliana* the pagan gods (*hlafordas, halgum* [lords, holy ones], *godu*, etc.) are contrasted with *soðne god, soðcyning*. And in *Azarias* 44–48, Azarias asks God to reveal his power so that the heathen may know "þæt þu ana eart . . . soð meotod [that you alone are the true lord]," and elsewhere in the poetry soð is one of the commonest epithets of the Christian God as distinguished from spurious heathen deities. In prose the word soð is also frequently used to contrast the Christian God with pagan gods. In Ælfric's and Wulfstan's interdependent homilies *De falsis diis*, pagan deities are differentiated from the God of Christendom, who is described as "se an soða god." In the Old English *Orosius*, soð is regularly used to differentiate the God of the Christians from heathen deities, as when the Egyptians are said to attribute certain miracles to "hiora agnum godum" and "nales þam soþan gode [to their own gods and not to the true God at all]," or when the Romans seek through sacrifices to recruit the help of their gods, who, says Orosius, "næs na se soða god." Even more familiar will be Bede's story of the conversion of Edwin, in which "þam soðan gode" and "þæs soðan godes" occur repeatedly to distinguish the Christian God of Paulinus from the pagan gods whom Cefi had worshiped. Here the term is a translation into Old English of Bede's *verus deus*, which in Christian Latin often serves to specify the Christian God. Gregory the Great uses it so in his letter to Abbot Mellitus, where the Pope contrasts the worship of God with the pagan Anglo-Saxons' worship of the devil.

The other epithet which the poet uses of God but which his characters never use is *self*. This too is a traditional way of distinguishing the God of Christendom from heathen gods, both in poetry and in prose, as in the twelfth *Vercelli Homily*, which says that when the pagans approached the idols which devils had occupied, "Þonne tealdon men þæt þæt wære god sylfa; wæron þæt þonne þa wyrrestan hellegæstas, nalas god sylfa, ælmihtig eallra gesceafta Scippend [Then people thought that it was God himself; yet they were the evilest of infernal creatures, by no means God himself, the almighty Creator of all creatures]." Similarly, Ælfric has St. Crysanthus contrast the powers of his Christian God with those of pagan idols: "Me fylste god sylf mid godcundre mihte. Þine godas ne geseoþ ne soðlice ne gehyrað ac syndon andgitlease mid leade gefæstnode [God himself supported me with divine power. Truly, your gods neither see nor hear, but are insensible and bound in lead]." Both *soð* and *sylf* are used in the Exeter Book *Maxims* where the poet is distinguishing between the pagan and Christian gods: "Woden worhte weos," he says, contrasting Woden with the ruler of the spacious heavens (*rume roderas*). Then he adds, "þæt is rice god, / sylf soðcyning, sawla nergend, /. . . þæt is meotud sylfa [Woden made idols . . . that is the God of power, the true King himself, the savior of souls, . . . that is God himself]" (133–37). The use of terms like *god sylf, soðcyning,* and *meotud sylfa* was, then, a common way of distinguishing God from false gods, and the *Beowulf* poet's use of them for this purpose reminds us of the ambiguous status of the terms for a higher being used by the heroes of the poem.

The reference in the Exeter *Maxims* to God as wielder of *rume roderas* introduces another means by which Anglo-Saxons specify the true God as opposed to pagan deities. In *Beowulf* only the poet refers to a God of the Heavens (*heofena helm* in 182, *rodera rædend* in 1555); his characters do not know the dwelling place of the true God, "for all the gods of the nations are idols, but the Lord made the heavens" (Psalm 96:5). Ignorance of where the true God dwells is a characteristic of the virtuous heathen that is noted by Snorri in his preface to the *Prose Edda*: "They knew not yet where his kingdom was; but this they believed: that he ruled all things on earth and in the sky." In Old English poems about Christians or Jews striving against heathens, "God of the heavens" is often used to specify the true God, and in later saints' lives the God who is "in heaven" is frequently so distinguished (possibly with an echo from the Lord's Prayer) from the false gods of the heathen. The *heofonlice* God is contrasted with the gods of the heathen in *De falsis diis* as well.

There are, then, distinctions between the theological language of the poet and that of his pagan characters, but the distinctions are deliberately muted by the preponderance of terms which are shared by the poet with his characters but which carry different meanings, depending on which of the two contexts applies. This is the poet's characteristic method for dealing with the theological tensions in the poem, and it bears further exemplification and analysis. In the two sentences foretelling the outcome of the fight with Grendel, the poet says,

> Ac him dryhten forgeaf
> wigspeda gewiofu,   Wedera leodum,
> frofor ond fultum,   þæt hie feond heora
> ðurh anes cræft   ealle ofercomon,
> selfes mihtum.   Soð is gecyþed,
> þæt mihtig god   manna cynnes
> weold wideferhð.

[But the Lord bestowed on the Storm-Geats webs of success in war, help and support, so that they overcame all their foes through the strength of One, through His own powers. The truth is manifest: mighty God has always ruled the race of men.]

(696–702)

Commentators have been eager to dismiss the overt pagan allusion *wig-speda gewiofu* [a web of victories], but it would seem to function here precisely according to the poet's usual strategy with theological language. From the perspective of Beowulf and his men, the victory they achieve will seem to be a woven web of destiny granted to them by a *dryhten*. But the poet knows that *dryhten* with a different meaning is the true source of their success, and that it is His help and support (*frofor ond fultum*) that give victory to the Geatas, although they cannot know it. The phrases *ðurh anes cræft* and *selfes mihtum* refer not, I suspect, to Beowulf, as is usually assumed, but to *dryhten, anes . . . selfes* carrying here that specialized meaning of "the one true God" discussed above. The poet implies here the familiar Augustinian notion that the true God has always ruled men's ways, helped and guided them, even when they did not know of Him:

> Soð is gecyþed,
> þæt mihtig god   manna cynnes
> weold wideferhð.

(700–2)

This important idea, which is expressed repeatedly at crucial points in *Beowulf,* is also seen in the Old English *Orosius,* where again and again it is urged that God's hand can be discerned in history, directing the affairs of men even when they were unaware of Him and sacrificing to idols. There is also something of the Boethian view here: what men in pre-Christian times took as the weavings of fate or wyrd was actually God's providence. Here again the poet contrives to gain dignity for his characters, suggesting that they were interacting with God and even enjoying His support, although they could not know it and were, of course, beyond His salvation.

We see the same double perspective in the sentence describing the thoughts of the Geatas as they await Grendel's attacks:

> Þæt wæs yldum cuþ,
> þæt hie ne moste, þa metod nolde,
> se s[c]ynscaþa under sceadu bregdan

[It was known to the men that the hostile demon could not fling them beneath the shades when the ruler did not wish it].

(705–7)

At the pre-Christian characters' level of perception, this is the Germanic warrior's familiar commonplace of grim consolation in mortal danger: like Sǫrli in *Hamðismál,* they knew that "no man outlives the evening after the Norns' decree," or, to state the sentiment positively, the men knew that they could not be killed if Fate had not ordained it. But the old heathen sense of *metod* (Fate, the Measurer) had been overlaid in Christian times by the meaning "Lord" (the Christian God), and poet and audience know that it is *metod* in this sense that was truly presiding over the conflict in the poem, determining whether the warriors should survive or die. In the past scholars have attended to only one level or the other of the sentence's meaning rather than to both, and as a result conflicting interpretations have resulted. A. J. Wyatt, for example, prints *metod* with a lowercase *m,* implying that he sees only the characters' understanding of the sentence, while Klaeber and others capitalize the first letter of *Metod,* signaling a Christian version of the statement. The Geatas' pre-Christian sense of the passage is a primitive, inchoate version of the full sense perceived by poet and audience in light of their fuller understanding gained through revelation. Both levels of perception are operative in the poem, but each must be appreciated in its proper context.

We see *metod* operating in this homonymous way in direct discourse as well as in reported speech. In his monologue before engaging the dragon, Beowulf says that the outcome of the battle shall be "swa unc wyrd geteoð, / metod manna gehwæs" (2526–27): "as wyrd, the measurer of each person, shall decree for us." This surely is the meaning that the words have for Beowulf, and editors like von Schaubert who specify that *metod* here means "fate" are clearly right. And yet Klaeber and others who insist that *metod* means "(Christian) God" are also right; they are simply viewing Beowulf's statement from the perspective of the narrating poet, for whom *metod manna gehwæs* could only seem like an appositive gloss to *wyrd,* explaining providentially the true nature of wyrd, which, as Christians knew, was but the accomplishment of God's determinations. "Metod eallum weold / gumena cynnes, swa he nu git deð [The ordainer of fate (the lord) ruled all of mankind then, as he still does now]," says the poet (1057–58), but *metod* has undergone a momentous semantic change since the time when He was presiding over the noble heathens of the tale of Beowulf, and this, I believe, poet and audience fully understood.

Aldhelm understands it when, in his seventh enigma, 3–4, he has a personified Fate say, "The Ancients falsely named me mistress, who swayed the scepter of the world until the Grace of God assumed command." In his verse tract on virginity, moreover, Aldhelm often uses pagan Classical epithets for the Deity, expecting his readers to recognize the Virgilian or Horatian origins of his verbal finery while simultaneously supplying the proper Christian referent, which the context of his treatise requires. This use of pre-Christian terminology for higher beings is perhaps more commonplace among Anglo-Saxons than we usually realize. Even in the Anglo-Saxon charters we find opening formulas like "in nomine altitonantis mundi satoris," "in nomine summi tonantis," and "ego Eadwig largiflua summi tonantis providentia rex Anglorum." And Christian-Latin poets like Arator and Prudentius, who were popular in Anglo-Saxon England, made similar use of terms like *tonans* and *numen* to refer to the Christian God even while using the same terms in the same works to refer to pagan gods. In one English manuscript of Arator and Prudentius, moreover, we actually encounter an Anglo-Saxon reader analyzing these classical terms for deities to distinguish places where the words refer to pagan gods from those where they refer to the Christian God: over forms of *tonans* (thunderer) and *numen* (divinity), he writes *deus, creator, verbum dei,* or *christus vel deus* when the terms refer to the Christian Deity, while superscribing *idola, fictiles dei,* or *dei vel simulacra* when the same terms refer to the false gods. These glosses show an

Anglo-Saxon reading a poetic text in just the way that I am suggesting *Beowulf* would have been read. Had the Cambridge glossator turned his attention to *Beowulf,* he might well have found himself pondering the same ambiguities that resulted when Arator and Prudentius use originally pagan terms for the Christian God, but in this case it would be pagan Germanic terms. But in applying his differentiating glosses to *Beowulf,* he would have to have decided whether he was viewing each god name from the perspective of the character who spoke it or from that of the poet who was putting the word in the character's mouth.

Reading *Beowulf* is, in a way, like reading the centos of Proba, Luxorius and Pomponius, who composed entire poems on Christian subjects by rearranging the verses of Virgil, Horace, and Ovid in order to make them convey Christian meanings. Students of these curious works hold two contexts in mind at the same time, for their pleasure is in following the Christian level of the narrative while remaining aware of the source of the poetic language. Just as in reading the centos we think simultaneously of Aeneas and Christ, so in reading *Beowulf* we should hear distant echoes of Thunor and Woden when the men of old appeal to their *mihtig dryhten* and *fæder alwalda.* We know to whom these words refer in the Christian present, but we also know that they once referred to other, darker beings.

The theological vocabulary of *Beowulf* undergoes a centolike transformation in reverse when the poet locates his story with its Christianized Germanic diction back in a pre-Christian, pre-Cædmonian era. It is quite simply the dramatic setting of the poem that reactivates the non-Christian meanings of words. And lest the audience be unmindful of these meanings, the poet at times builds into his text reminders of pre-Christian meanings by using words in contexts which delimit their semantic range to exclusively pre-Christian reference. In the compound *metodsceaft* [decree of fate], used once by Wealhtheow and once by the dying Beowulf, *metod* can only mean "fate," and the simplex *metod* in 2527 is forced to have a predominantly pagan meaning because it is placed in apposition to *wyrd.* These usages of the word, occurring alongside usages in which the sense is clearly and exclusively the Christianized one (e.g., 110, 1057), ensure that when readers encounter the word in statements like Beowulf's comment "Ic hine ne mihte, þa metod nolde, / ganges getwæman [I could not, when metod did not wish it / keep him from going]," they will have both meanings in mind and will understand that the one meaning fits the world of the dramatic speaker, while another is suggested to the Christian audience. Should they fail to respond to the play of double sense in this passage, the poet adds a further jog to memory, stating in 1611, "þæt is soð metod." This reminds us overtly that there is a true Christian metod as well as a false pre-Christian metod in question and that we must keep both in mind.

Again, when Hrothgar says in 945 that *ealdmetod* was favorable to Beowulf's mother when she bore him, he is thinking no doubt of "the ancient measurer, the ancient dispenser," or simply "fate." To a Christian hearing the word, however, it would carry the further meaning "God of old." In the peculiar context of *Beowulf,* moreover, the word may well have suggested a third and troubling import: Hrothgar has indeed invoked the "old" metod in contrast to the new metod. Such interplay of significations comes easily in *Beowulf* not only because the poet restricts his God terminology so carefully but also because of the appositive style. The ubiquitous variations playing off one term against the other, activating one meaning of a word in one passage and another in a different passage, tease us into a constant alertness to the semantic layering of words, much as Shakespeare's puns and quibbles attune his audience's ears to the more serious resonances of Elizabethan English. . . .

As D. H. Green reminds us [in *The Carolingian Lord*], several scholars have noted the analogy between the Christianization of the Old English vocabulary and the early missionaries' conversion of pagan shrines to Christian uses, following the advice that Pope Gregory gave to Abbot Mellitus. The analogy is sound, for in both renovations the result is a fusion of Christian with pre-Christian elements: Anglo-Saxon Christianity supersedes the old lore but is content to subsist with echoes from the past. The accommodation of the two could go awry, as when King Rædwald erected within the same temple one altar to Christ and another to the old pagan gods. If disproportions occur in the Christian-pagan accommodation in the poetic language, it is probably in the opposite direction of underemphasizing the pagan element, at least in the diction of *Beowulf.* For at times the poet, in his efforts to lend dignity to the heroes' piety, seems to err on the side of Christianizing their piety. Once Beowulf refers to *ecum dryhtne* (2796), and a modern reader might object that the gods of the Northmen, so far as we can tell from Icelandic sources, were mortal, not *ece* (i.e., "eternal"). But such an objection would probably impart to the adjective *ece* a specificity which is unwarranted. In Ælfric's first letter to Wulfstan, *ece* describes the material to be used for making a chalice and apparently means simply "lasting, durable." In *Exodus* 370 *ece lafe* is the "lasting remnant" on Noah's ark, the specimens of the various creatures from which postdiluvian generations will spring. In the Old English *Orosius, ece* modifies *þeowas* where we are told that the Samnites wanted to make the Romans their perpetual slaves or their slaves for life. In *Paris Psalter* 64:9, *eceum wæstmum* appears to mean "lasting fruits," while *ece gear* in 76:5 means "years of old" ("of yore, of old" being one of the senses of the *Vulgate aeternus*). In *Beowulf, ece* modifies *eorðreced,* the dragon's lair. Beowulf's *ecum dryhtne* in 2796, then, may have meant nothing more to the dying hero than "the enduring prince" or "the prince of old." It is only with Cædmonization of the vocabulary that *ece dryhten* assumes the unvarying sense of "eternal Lord."

Tolkien was troubled by the phrase "godes leoht geceas" (2469), spoken by Beowulf as he recounts the death of Hrethel. Are these words wholly inappropriate in the mouth of a pre-Christian Geat? In both Old English and Old Icelandic *leoht* (OIcel. *ljós*) can have the metaphorical sense of "a region or condition." An expression for "to die" is "fara í ljós annat," (go to the other region or condition). Beowulf's comment "gumdream ofgeaf, godes leoht geceas" could be simply a variation of the standard periphrasis, carrying the meaning "he left the joys of men and sought out the realm of a god." We might even take the expression literally, if Icelandic mythology is to be trusted as a representation of general Germanic beliefs about the next world. *Vǫluspá* 64:2 tells us that the hall Gimlé, which is *sólu fegra* (brighter than the sun), is where good men shall go after death, and Snorri reiterates the point in the *Prose Edda*. Other halls of the gods are also described as brilliant with light, *Breidablik,* meaning "broad-gleaming," and *Glitnir,* meaning "glittering." And the light elves are prominent in the realm of the Norse gods. Since the poet's strategy seems to be to dwell on those aspects of pre-Christian beliefs which are least in conflict with Christian culture, it is possible that he chose "godes leoht geceas" as a phrase which could be justified in terms of Germanic pagan mythology while at the same time having, by happy chance, a certain Christian resonance.

A more complex case is that of Old English *dom*. This is at once a most Christian and a most pagan word. When the poet says in his own voice, "Swa hit oð domes dæg diope benemdon / þeodnas mære [Thus lords of renown had laid a heavy curse on it until the day of doom]" (3069–70), we may be fairly sure that in the poet's mind *domes dæg* refers to the purely Christian concept of the Last Judgment. But elsewhere the word *dom* is used eleven times with the earlier meaning "fame"—the (good) judgment which is passed on men's deeds by posterity and which affords a man the only life beyond death he can be sure of in a pagan world. Beowulf articulates this view most clearly when he says,

> wyrce se þe mote
> domes ær deaþe;   þæt bið drihtguman
> unlifigendum   æfter selest.

[let him who may achieve fame before his death; that is the best thing for the warrior who is no longer alive.]

(1387–89)

Three times it is used in another traditional Germanic sense: Beowulf, Sigemund, and Wiglaf on different occasions each receive a reward of treasure according to *selfes dom* ("their own judgment")—that is, the maximum amount. In all these occurrences the meaning of *dom* poses no difficulty. Twice, however, Beowulf uses the word in contexts which have been taken by some readers to be references to the Last Judgment— a problematic reading, since the pre-Christian hero could have had no knowledge of Christian eschatology. In 977–79, Beowulf says that when the wounded Grendel returns to the mere, there in his cave he must await "miclan domes, hu him scir metod scrifan wille." Earlier Beowulf had said that when he and Grendel fought, the loser, who dies, will have to accept *dryhtnes dome* (441). Contrary to prevailing opinion, I do not believe that these are references to the Last Judgment. Rather Beowulf is saying that combatants who suffer defeat have to resign themselves to the de- cision of the god who determines when people shall die. A similar idea is expressed by Beowulf in 685–86, where he says that if Grendel joins battle with him, then

> witig god
> on swa hwæþere hond   halig dryhten
> mærðo deme,   swa him gemet þince.
> (685–87)

That is, the wise god, the divine lord, will assign the glory of victory on whichever side seems to him proper. In Old Icelandic literature *dómr* often refers to the decision of a higher (pagan) power as to when a person shall die. We see this sense in the compound *Norna-dómr*, the decision of the three Norns who control both the fate of the world and the individual fate of each man. *Skapa-dómr*, "the judgment of fate," has a similar sense. In poetry this usage yielded a formula for "to die"—*njóta Norna dóms* (to undergo the judgment of the Norns). When Beowulf says, then, that Grendel, after his defeat, "must await the great decision as to what the manifest ordainer will decree for him," he would appear to be using a Germanic formula for dying. (It would seem pointless to say he must wait to see how he fares in the Last Judgment, since the poet has been specific and repetitive in asserting Grendel's sure damnation.) Similarly, when Beowulf says before the combat that the loser will have to resign himself to the doom of the lord, he is saying what any Germanic warrior might appropriately say. The poet's Christian audience might well be reminded of Christian Doomsday by these death formulas of Beowulf's, but they would not assume that Beowulf would be aware of this overtone. Rather they would probably feel pity for a noble heathen who faces death without true understanding of what that death means.

The discussion thus far has centered largely on the polysemous nature of the *Beowulf* poet's terms for God and God's determinations, but the same semantic layering of Christian and pre-Christian senses is present in much of the poetic language at large. Sometimes the context activates one sense, sometimes another, but in all cases the apposed meanings are present *in posse,* and each time the audience privileges one meaning of a word and suppresses another, it is reminded of the theological contrast between itself and the characters in the poem, for that contrast has been incorporated into the poetic language itself. The word *mægen,* for example, had both Christian and non-Christian meanings in Old English. Modern editors in their glossaries tell us that the only meaning the word has in *Beowulf* is "strength, might," since these are the qualities the hero needs in his struggles with men and monsters. But I wonder whether the minds of Anglo-Saxons listening to *Beowulf* were as linguistically compartmentalized as an editor's glossary. To a Christian Anglo-Saxon, *mægen* was a single word with a single continuum of meanings. The basic sense was "physical strength," but there are derived senses relating to various kinds of power, including the Christian sense "virtue" (a development parallel to that in the Latin *virtus* as it was used by Christian Latin writers). Since the Christian sense "virtue" had become a part of the word's meaning, presumably the audience of *Beowulf* could not but feel the presence of that sense even when it encountered *mægen* referring to physical strength. And each time the listeners' minds registered the irrelevance of the Christian sense, there was a momentary, flickering recognition of the fact that the noble race whose deeds they were admiring was, after all, distanced from the audience by a gulf of tragic ignorance.

An important, recurrent expression of the *Beowulfian* narrative perspective is the statement that the hero "wæs moncynnes mægenes strengest / on þæm dæge þysses lifes (He was of all mankind the strongest in strength (*mægen*) in *that* day of *this* life) (196–97; cf. 789–90, 806). As Roberta Frank has now observed, the temporal distance between pagan past and Christian present is skillfully emphasized by the abnormal alliterative stress on *þam* and *þysses*. Less skillful, we might think, is the apparent tautology "strongest in strength." But consideration of the apposed meanings "strength" and "virtue" which inhere in *mægen* may lead us to a fuller appreciation of this half-line. Remembering that the word which could mean "Christian virtue" to the audience meant only "physical strength" in Beowulf's day, we may suspect that, to a contemporary of the poet's, the sentence could have meant something like "He was of all mankind the strongest in what passed for virtue in that day of this life." Only for the characters in the poem would there have been a tautology; for poet and audience the increment of meaning which the word *mægen* had attained by their day would have made *mægenes strengest* significantly contrastive, especially with the following line "on þæm dæge þysses lifes," emphasizing the two distinct periods of Anglo-Saxon history.

The numerous subsequent occurrences of *mægen* would have had something of the same dual significance. When Hrothgar, proclaiming Beowulf's fitness for kingship, says to the young hero, "þu eart mægenes strang ond on mode frod [you are mighty in strength/virtue and wise in spirit]," the audience, perceiving the nontautological sense of the phrase, recognizes that Beowulf *is* virtuous as well as strong in Hrothgar's sense, but he is lacking in awareness of his virtue's source and nature. Again, Wiglaf says of Beowulf's desperate predicament on his death-day, "Nu is se dæg cumen / þæt ure mandryhten mægenes behofað [Now is the day come / that our lord has need of strength/virtue]" (2646–47). To the poem's audience, Wiglaf says more than he realizes: Beowulf's death day is indeed the day when he has need of Christian virtue. But since he exercises his prowess on the far side of the semantic change which gave Christian meaning to *mægen*, Beowulf's greatest need cannot possibly be met.

In an earlier passage *maegen* interacts with another word which has both Christian and pre-Christian meanings. Explaining how Beowulf prevailed in the fight with Grendel, the poet says, "He gemunde mægenes strenge, / gimfæste gife, ðe him god sealde [He remembered the power of his strength, / the ample gift that (a) god had bestowed on him]"

(1270–71). In pre-Christian times *gife* meant "gift," pure and simple, but with Christianization of the vocabulary it came to serve simultaneously as the common term for Christian grace. While Beowulf, with his pre-Christian meanings, thinks that the only gift that a god has given him is his physical strength, the Christian audience knows that the real gift that God offers is grace, and that grace, if understood, enables a person to recognize and practice the virtue requisite for salvation. The poet repeats this interplay of meanings in lines 670 and 2182, exploiting there the double sense of *hyldo* and *metod* as well as of *mægen*.

Words like *mægen*, in which dual semantic layers are activated by the dual perspectives in the poem, illustrate that the play of double sense in *Beowulf* is not simply a matter of recalling pre-Christian senses of words but also of bringing to a reader's experience of the poem the Christian meanings which developed after the period of the poem's present time. If we read *Beowulf* bearing in mind its diction's full range of meaning, compounds and phrases like *mægencræft* and *mægenes cræft*, *mægenstrengo* and *mægenes strenge*, all of which have been designated "tautological" compounds or phrases, are invested with contrastive meaning and a slight situational irony by the dual perspectives in the poem.

The early need for an Anglo-Saxon vocabulary of iniquity in the Christian context also led to words of dual meaning. Two high-frequency words meaning "sin, wickedness" which give a strong tone of Christian condemnation to certain actions of characters in the poem are *synn* and *firen*. For Christian Anglo-Saxons who read the poem, there can be little doubt that the condemnatory tone is there, but the *Beowulf* poet also uses each of these words at least once in the poem with its original, pre-Christian meaning. *Synn* before the conversion meant simply "hostility," and *firen* meant "pain, violence." The *fyrenþearf* suffered by the Danes at the beginning of the poem (14) could not possibly be "sinful need"; it is "painful need"; and the *synn ond sacu* of the Swedish wars (2472) is "hostility and strife," not "sin," just as the *fæhðe ond fyrene* in the same context (2480) would mean "enmity and violence." Having been reminded in these passages of the early, nontheological meaning of these words, the audience would realize when it encountered them in other contexts that, for pre-Christian people like the characters in the poem, the Christian meanings would not have been operative. The Swedes and Geatas of *Beowulf* would have been innocent of the theological dimensions of their violent behavior: what is "wickedness" to the poet's audience was simply pain and strife to them. This contrast of apposed Christian-pagan senses is especially clear in *bealu* and its compounds.

Most editors indicate that the central meaning of *bealu* in the poem is "evil." But this is a late signification assigned to the word by Christian reformers of the vocabulary. The primitive sense was "aggression, attack, torment," and this meaning is dominant in compounds like *bealohycgend* (applied to both Beowulf and the dragon in 2565), *feorhbealu, sweordbealu,* and *wigbealu*. Klaeber's glosses like "deadly evil" and "sword evil" for the *-bealu* compounds represent the senses that a perceptive audience of the poem might briefly entertain and then reject as the context in *Beowulf* reminds them of the more relevant pre-Christian senses of *-bealu*. The early sense is especially important when a pagan character uses the word. When Beowulf says, "Ic mid elne sceall / gold gegangan, oððe guð nimeð, / feorhbealu frecne frean eowerne [I shall by valor / attain the gold, or else battle, mortal aggression, will take your king]" (2535–37), he is not pronouncing war to be "a deadly evil." The relevant sense is the one suggested by the appositive *guð*—"mortal aggression." Similarly in 2250 *feorhbealu* stands in apposition with *guðdeað,* a precise chiastic equivalent. *Bealocwealm* in 2265 means "death from attack" (cf. *beaducwealm, wælcwealm* [violent death]); *bealu-* here is not, as Klaeber says "more or less devoid of distinct meaning." Again the poet forces us to assign the word its primitive, concrete meaning in 2826, where the dragon is said to have been *bealwe gebæded*—"pressed by (Beowulf's) attack." If we ignore such reminders as this and the appositives, which constantly emphasize the pre-Christian sense of *bealu,* then we shall impute to the characters in the poem an attitude toward battle and heroic contention which may well have been a part of the Christian world view of poet and audience but which would have been wholly out of keeping with the culture of the men of old in their relentless quest for *dom ær deaðe*.

The semantic stratification of Old English poetic diction in Christian times is precisely what the *Beowulf* poet needed to articulate the tensions felt by a people who might say (as Ælfric says in a different context) that they were "of hæðenum magum, æþelborenum swaðeah, of wurðfulre mægðe æfter woruldþingum [of heathen kindred, but nobly born and of a stock glorious according to things of this world]." These people would find it hard to renounce a heritage as glorious as theirs, even though they acknowledge that it is glorious only "æfter woruldþingum." The *Beowulf* poet's subtle use of apposed word meanings is one means by which he builds a place for the Germanic heroic world in the collective memory of his Christian nation. It is the means also by which he supplies a moving, negative response, as it were, to that simplistic Christian attitude toward ancient pagan heroism stated by Pascal: "Les exemples des morts généreuses de Lacédémoniens et autres ne nous touchent guère. Car qu'est-ce que cela nous apporte? Mais l'exemple de la mort des martyrs nous touche; car ce sont 'nos membres.' Nous avons un lien commun avec eux. . . . Il n'est rien de cela aux exemples des païens: nous n'avons point de liaison à eux [The examples of the noble deaths of the Lacedemonians and others hardly touch us. For what does it mean to us? But the example of the death of martyrs touches us, for they are 'our own.' We have a common bond with them. . . .There is none of that in the pagans' examples: we have no relation with them]."

The author of *Beowulf* is not the only English epic poet who has used the peculiar resources of his native tongue to effect a theological accommodation in his audience's world view. In *Paradise Lost* John Milton exploits dual meanings of words to suggest conflicting perspectives in his account of the Fall of Man. As Arnold Stein, Christopher Ricks, and others have observed, Milton often employs Latin-derived English words with their original Latin word meanings rather than with their conventional English meanings, particularly in parts of the poem devoted to describing Paradise before the Fall. Thus when he describes how dutiful the sun and stars are in shining upon Adam and Eve, Milton does not use the words "dutiful" or "obedient" but rather says that the heavenly bodies are "obsequious" and "officious." In Latin these words carried the innocent meaning "obliging, dutiful," and this is the meaning required by context. But in Milton's English, as in ours today, the words had come to have the pejorative senses "fawning" and "meddlesome." The rivers of Paradise are described as flowing "in mazy error" with "liquid lapse of murm'ring streams," and the reader must supply the Latin meanings "wandering" for "error" and "sliding" or "flowing" for "lapse" (Latin *lapsus*) while remaining aware that, during the time since the words "error" and "lapse" had been borrowed into English, they had developed the negative senses "mistake" and "failing" (cf. "prelapsarian" and "postlapsarian," where "lapse" refers specifically to the Fall of Man). This pattern of bilingual play on words of Latin origin gives the reader a sense of two historical stages in the language Milton is using, a prelapsarian stage when the Latinate words still had their pristine, innocent meanings and a postlapsarian stage when they had developed their pejorative English meanings. Each time he encounters one of these words in Milton's descriptive language, the reader is reminded that he is rooted in postlapsarian time, speaking a fallen language with sullied, vernacular meanings, while for our first parents in Paradise the same words had the pure and wholesome meanings expressive of the paradisal state. Thus, in a psychologically effective way Milton forces the language of his epic to express, through its semantic stratification, a major motif of the poem.

The use of apposed word meanings in *Beowulf* serves the Anglo-Saxon poet's purposes in a similar way. In both cases the poet's language does not merely communicate but rather enacts the meaning of a heroic narrative concerned with man's theological fate. In Milton the polysemous words add poignancy to the poet's backward gaze from postlapsarian time to the happy era before the Fall, while the *Beowulf* poet uses his homonymous diction to suggest the perspective of one gazing back from the time of redemption to the era when men had no hope. But since Milton's device is based upon a more or less accidental linguistic phenomenon (the fact that many seventeenth-century English words happen to have been derived from Latin), it cannot be as intimately cooperative with his poem's theme and perspective as is the *Beowulf* poet's handling of his consistently polysemous diction. By keeping alive, through context and grammatical apposition, both primitive meanings and post-Cædmonian meanings of his traditional poetic language, the *Beowulf* poet forces us to see in the very language of his people living relics of their nation's religious history. Amid the historically determined ambiguities of his Cædmonian formulas, the poet finds a place in his people's mind and language where their ancestors can remain, not with theological security, but with dignity. For, by remaining true to the heroic ideal of *pietas* (or *treowþ*), the men of old came as close as possible to Christian piety; by honoring metod in the primitive sense, they were, unawares, simulating their descendants' faith in Metod in the new, Christian sense. But the poet, in his honesty, never suggests that such simulation, such groping toward true piety, is sufficient for salvation. For that a person must have revelation. A poet cannot save lost souls with poetry, but in the rich imbrications of Old English poetic diction, this poet recognized a powerful emblem of his people's tragic past, and by exploiting these apposed meanings of words in the traditional vocabulary, he was able to vest each line of his poem with deep significance, adding to his celebration of ancestral valor a compassionate tone of Christian regret.

Epitaphs for Æglæcan: Narrative Strife in *Beowulf*

Ian Duncan

> *Whoever fights monsters should take care that in the process he does not become a monster. And when you look long into an abyss, the abyss looks back into you.*
>
> NIETZSCHE

The poem called *Beowulf* stands as monumental and solitary as its hero's barrow over the time-levelled scene of Old English literature. For those benighted voyagers who would find their way by the poem's beacon, that splendid uniqueness poses problems. We have almost no coordinates of tradition or convention—not even fixed historical coordinates of time and place of production—by which we may check our responses to the poem. Arguments for any interpretation of *Beowulf* have therefore described discursive configurations within the poem which have then been projected outside it to map, explicitly or otherwise, such a context of tradition, genre, ethos, Weltanschauung. The trouble is that the less aware the critic that this is his procedure, the more likely is he to be not "finding" but forming those very intratextual orders by projecting into the poem his own historical assumptions or the contemporary ideological and generic habits of his own reading. Thus we have had, variously, *Beowulf* as epic (timeless genre of heroic aspiration); *Beowulf* as Christian allegory; *Beowulf* as the foundation of a uniquely "English" tradition of sensibility, fortuitously excavated on the eve of historic nationalism; *Beowulf* as a sophisticated meditation on the glamour and fatal limitations of an old Germanic pagan ethos; and so forth.

One way of responding to the challenge of reading the poem—how do we apprehend its strangeness, leave its otherness intact, not familiarize it utterly—is to look for a dynamic of genres and discourses within the text, testing and measuring one another, rather than seek to homogenize the whole text into some imaginary generic monolith. Everyone agrees that the poem consists of a series of combats between a hero and a monster, alternating with so-called digressions on historical and dynastic subject matter. Structurally speaking, the monster-fight series is the repetition of a single narrative unit or genre. Of course, the repetition is progressive, or incremental, although critics have disagreed in what way, and we might begin by considering the nature of this progress: the kinds of shifts that take place in the monster fight throughout the poem, and the textual pressures behind and around those shifts.

Perhaps the central interpretive claim for *Beowulf* is that the monsters are "evil" and the hero "good," and that the poem is articulated by a thematic conflict between good and evil, as if these were transcendental categories immediately available for all poets and readers. No such categorical master terms, however, are used in the poem, but a varied range of epithets that we cannot simply boil down to ethical essences. J. R. R. Tolkien, in an essay that set the terms for a metaphysical-allegorical reading of the poem (and his own remains one of the strongest and most careful of such readings), provides a commentary on the terms used to describe Grendel, and detects a cultural sensibility poised over the shift from a primitive, animistic rendering (Grendel as flesh-and-blood ogre in the wilderness) toward a more modern and symbolical imagination (a "diabolizing" rhetoric which deploys such tags as *feond mancynnes* [mankind's enemy], *Godes andsaca* [God's adversary]).

Let us, for the moment, follow Tolkien in keeping the monsters with the hero at the center of our concern, and in trying to interpret their adversary situation there. A combat between a hero and a monster is as archetypal a narrative topos as one can find; specific analogues to the troll and dragon fights in *Beowulf* have been recorded by Panzer and Aarne/Thompson in hundreds of folktales from all over the world, as well as in a number of the Norse sagas. What is most striking about the *Beowulf* treatment, and a sign of the poem's "literariness" compared with these analogues, is its dense and specific representation of a social world (or historical class) and its codes and values, against which the "evil" of the monsters is activated. The abominable *mearcstapan* [boundary-stalkers] and the dragon devastate the social fabric of the Danish and Geatish courts. Grendel invades Heorot, synecdoche for a social order at its balmiest:

> þæt þæs sele stande,
> reced selesta   rinca gehwylcum
> idel ond unnyt

[(sea travelers say) that this hall stands, / best of buildings, to all warriors / idle and useless].

(ll. 411–13)

Heorot under Grendel's night-sway is like the hoard under the dragon's guard, *eldum . . . unnyt* [useless to man] (3168). The monsters inflict a paralysis and evacuation of the system of exchange and mediation upon which the poem's courtly society constructs and codifies itself. Grendel drives Hrothgar and his men from their *gifstol* [treasure seat], while the dragon destroys Beowulf outright. Yet there is an inevitable dialectic of equivalence inscribed within this antithetical opposition. The ambiguity of the following crux seems to be calculated to suggest that Grendel infects the Danes with his own contagion:

> no he þone gifstol   gretan moste,
> maþðum for Metode,   ne his myne wisse.

[nor might he approach the treasure seat, / because of the Measurer, nor know his mind.]

(168–69)

Violating the social code, the Grendels extend, reverse, and parody it, to redefine themselves more fatally within its limits, but also it within theirs. If Grendel himself must always be defined as other, outside, and elsewhere to Heorot, bound to the obsession of his own negativity and lack, eternal outlaw and *ellorgæst* [alien spirit], then Hrothgar stands equally in need of a Grendel to define himself and Heorot. He recognizes that Grendel has been his divinely prescribed *edwenden* or nemesis. The poet's early prophecy of the destruction of Heorot by "se ecghete aþumsweoran [which] æfter wælniðe wæcnan scolde [sword hate between son-in-law and father-in-law (which) will awaken after murderous rage]" (84–85) rhetorically generates (*wæcnan*) Grendel himself, as a figure for that *ecghete/wælnið* which is self-destructively built into the dynastic codes of exchange and inheritance. The Creation song awakens his invasion because his own Cain genealogy continues, parodies, and completes it ("þanon untydras ealle onwocon [from thence an evil brood all awoke]" [111]).

Grendel's condition of captivity to his antithetical terms of otherness and lack is most powerfully figured as a *homelessness*. If Chambers and other commentators have cited English place names ("moras . . . fen ond fæsten [moors . . . fen and fastnesses]" [103–4]) after Grendel, his fate is nonetheless to be a *genius loci* without a *locus*. He is requited with a series of drastic separations (arm, soul, "deeds," head) which confirm his bondage ("þær him hel onfeng [there hell seized him]" [852]), but his condition has always been one of dismemberment. Cain is the first man without a community, an "atol angengea [horrid solitary one]" who contends "ana wið eallum [one against all]." If his exclusion defines the limits of the community, it also inscribes an equivalence with the antagonist who meets him on the community's behalf: at first a potential equivalence, but disturbingly activated as the poem proceeds. In his formal petition to Hrothgar, Beowulf sets out the terms under which he will encounter Grendel: he will "ana gehegan / ðing wið þyrse [alone carry out this affair against the demon]" (425–26), "ana (ond) minra eorla gedryht . . . Heorot fælsian [alone (with) my band of earls . . . (may) purge Heorot]" (431–32). The latter phrase captures the precarious ambiguity of the hero's exceptionality, his relationship to the social fabric he champions, which will have disintegrated by the end of the poem: severed from his *eorla gedryht*, he will be *an æfter eallum* [alone after all] (2268).

For the moment, however, the Heorot scenes allow us to witness the social machinery in magnificent working order, even though we are reminded of its fragility: the peace-weaving will fail to disconnect the imperative to feud. Beowulf comes, a stranger, to save the gift-seat from another stranger; his arrival makes up a buoyant narrative of the stately and exquisite performance of an elaborate system of mediations, the symbolic exchange of a delicate burden of challenges, namings, petitions, vows, and requitals among himself, the Coastguard, Wulfgar, Hrothgar, and Unferth, whose flyting forms a decorous link in the series. While the system of Scylding *sibbegedriht* [band of kinsmen] proscribes Grendel, it expands to accommodate Beowulf: with the final cutting-off of the trolls, the violation has been contained and the whole world is made kin. What we witness in this part of the poem is an idealizing harmonious coincidence of human wills with one another and with the narrative of the poem, allowed, directed, and calibrated by the regulations of a social code.

Yet we know from early on that this ideal moment of poise and fullness is transient (and Hrothgar and Beowulf seem to know it too), and that the fall of Heorot is inscribed in the social order it monumentalizes. While the issues of the Grendel affair, the *ðing wið þyrse*, are carefully established and contained by a procession of ritual speech-act exchanges, the *aglæcwif* [female monster] sequel, although (ironically) provided for by the code (she is avenging her son), must be responded to *ad hoc*, with an extemporization of the appropriate rituals. The dragon conflict (apart from opacities due to textual damage) is initiated without any sense of a stable support system of social codes to accommodate what is going on. Gone is Beowulf's assurance in the wherefore of the *sið* [venture], defined by containing social forms:

> wende se wisa,   þæt he Wealdende
> ofer ealde riht   ecean Dryhtne
> bitre gebulge;   breost innan weoll
> þeostrum geþoncum,   swa him geþywe ne wæs

[the wise one thought, that he the Ruler / over the old law (right), the eternal Lord, / had bitterly offended; the breast welled within him / with gloomy thoughts, as was not customary to him].

(2329–32)

The movement is clear enough: each time the monster strikes closer, the behaviour of the hero's companions deteriorates toward its folklore paradigm of treachery or desertion. This shift also affects the status of monster and hero: as the social machinery withers away, Beowulf and the dragon stand apart from it, both of them more radically alone. After Grendel, the monsters become increasingly self-reliant and self-sufficient creatures who hold sway over their own (albeit usurped) parody-halls which Beowulf must invade to confront them. The poet grants the dragon a certain elemental and sublime capacity to exult in his jealous mastery of earth-hall and air, far removed from Grendel's violent misery at his own existential hollowness, so that the elegy for the dead hero extends to accommodate his foe:

> lyftwynne heold
> nihtes hwilum,   nyðer eft gewat
> dennes niosian;   wæs ða deaðe fæst,
> hæfde eorðscrafa   ende genyttod.

[(he) held joy of air / formerly at nighttime, came back down /

to seek his den; then he was made fast by death, / had of his
earth-cave enjoyed the end.]

(3043–46)

His alienness to the human community he attacks is more radical than
Grendel's, for it is not constructed by a simple antithesis to which he is
bound. While Grendel is defined by his violation of the law which proscribes him, the dragon holds to, even embodies a law more primeval
than the social: "Draca sceal on hlæwe; frod, frætwum wlanc [a dragon
must be in a cave, old and wise, glorying in treasures]," as the convention
is elsewhere neatly summarized. That which compels the dragon to
avenge the plundered cup, just as it compelled him to nose out the hoard
in the first place, carries at least as much force as whatever *ræd* [counsel]
guides Beowulf's *sið*. We are dealing no longer with a personal blood
feud, but with a property feud, and the dragon's hoard concretizes the
strong sense of impersonality which pervades this final episode.

Just as the dragon's apartness seems unaccommodated by a weak-
ened system of social terms, so Beowulf's exceptional individuality in
the Grendel episodes has grown into a more essential and ominous isolation. The narratives of his escape as the last survivor of Higelac's raid,
earm anhaga [wretched solitary one] (2368), and of his childhood, establish this isolation as a characterological condition. Always an ambiguous
figure at Higelac's court (and the poet, typically, seems to play upon that
ambiguity by withholding the information about Higelac's reluctance for
his Denmark expedition and about his slack youth, which contradict the
impression we have received early in the poem), Beowulf will be radically
alone at the end, save for the companionship of another ambiguously
situated young man, Wiglaf. One constant of the dynastic narratives in
this poem seems to be that the transmission of social power is never
unproblematical; Beowulf's solitude will have terrible consequences for
the dynastic history that must resume after his death. As is notorious,
the one who is closest to Beowulf at the end is his antagonist: both are
described as *æglæcan* [monsters], and the dragon's dying gesture is to
greet the hero with a parodic repetition of the parting salute of old Hrothgar:

> Gecyste þa   cyning æþelum god,
> þeoden Scyldinga   ðegn betstan
> ond be healse genam

[Then the king of good descent kissed / the king of the Scyldings, the best of thanes, / grasped him by the neck].

(1870–72)

[fyrdraca] . . . ræsde on ðone rōfan,   þa him rum ageald,
hat ond heaðogrim,   heals ealne ymbefeng
biteran banum

[(the firedragon) . . . rushed on the brave one when opportunity allowed, / hot and battlegrim, enclosed all around his neck / with sharp fangs].

(2690–92)

Nobody's will or understanding coincides with or controls the narrative in this last part of the poem, a disjunction always underlying the earlier parts but then negotiated by the mediation of social codes and conventions which have by now crumbled away.

Yet the pressure of the historic-dynastic narrative upon the mythological-monster narrative has grown as the poem progresses, and by the end a radical shift in their relations (always already there, however) has made itself felt. I wish now to bring forward the argument I suggested initially, that if we are not permitted to understand *Beowulf* in terms of a tradition or genre which embraces the whole poem, we can understand it nevertheless as constituted by a contest or interplay of different genres within the text, arena for a Bakhtinian *heteroglossia*. This argument owes much to John Leyerle's powerful trope for the poem's formal principle, *interlace*. Agreeing with him that "there are no digressions in Beowulf," I suggest at the risk of excessive abstraction that the poem is largely governed by the interaction of two different narrative genres which represent different (antithetical) epistemological and interpretive modes. The monstrous and dynastic elements must be read in dynamic, constantly shifting relation to one another. The nineteenth century wanted a heroic poem disembarrassed of monsters, while Tolkien valorized the monsters to the exclusion of much else, and recent commentary has tended to read the "digressions" as supporting or filling out the poem's so-called "organic unity" (*i.e.,* they thematically or metaphorically underwrite the central allegory of Pride, etc.). The three monster fights (and their analogues and repetitions within the poem) propose a linear, chronological, "transparent" narrative, enjoying a mythologically univocal closure: good hero slays evil monster, saves the world. While the generic shape of the narrative would be known to the audience, specific movements of how and wherefore would not, the articulation between these two levels generating what we call "suspense." The historical-genealogical material, on the other hand, is narrated through a rhetoric of allusion, in a calculated refusal of chronological linearity for a labyrinthine involution which represents the treacherous crossings and entanglements (*inwitnet*

[net of malice], *searoniðas* [treacherous quarrels]) of its subject matter of dynastic feud. It is a narrative which deconstructs a teleological generic shape, perpetuating itself in a relentless etiology and governed by a characteristic trope of *edwenden,* hidden contradictions, and reversals which emerge in time, and which can only be known about as *chronicle*—by special knowledge on the part of an audience after the event. Unlike the monster fight, there is little room for suspense, for the shape of the narrative can only be seen afterwards as facts and names have determined it. While the monster fight proposes a narrative mastery over time in its teleological closure, the dynastic narrative, never standing still, always self-destabilizing, demonstrates its temporal determination.

As we have seen, the early part of the poem seeks to hold these narrative modes in suspension, to contain their mutual antagonism, by the mediation of the machinery of social codes and meanings. Thus, the Grendel fight is offered as a symbolic (mythological) resolution of the tensions and contradictions of its context of historical reality. Grendel is a scapegoat who externalizes the treachery and murder-bale of the community, and Beowulf cleanses (*fælsian*) Heorot in an act of exorcism. In other words, the relationship between the two narrative modes proposes itself as a dialectic, in which the monster fight represents the symbolic resolution of the historical contradictions of the social world. But (and this is where the poem is so powerful) such resolution remains only symbolic, and thus limited, as we are made aware early on: Grendel, the descendant of Cain, may be destroyed, but the real heritage of Cain, and indeed the heritage of the Fall and of the Creation itself which rhetorically "awakens" him for the narrative, is the secret *ecghete,* historical necessity in the hearts of men, which remains inscribed within the order of things at Heorot. This knowledge creeps forward as the poem proceeds: the poet's description of the third night at Heorot seems to nudge us toward an anticipation of a further supplement to the Grendelkin raids, undoing the closure of the monster purging. But the *untydras* [evil broods] lurk within Heorot: the sequel is indeed prepared for.

Thus, what would be a mutually confirming narrative dialectic in the early part of the poem begins to break down as the rich texture of social decorum covering, binding, and patterning the poem's world thins and frays. We feel that Higelac is insubstantial, his court small-time, after Hrothgar and Heorot, and what is noteworthy about Beowulf's own repetition of the monster fight narrative is that he foregrounds the reader's growing unease about the tension between the narrative and the historical narrative *de rebus gestis Danorum,* held in check during the first part of the poem: the two modes now resist one another, and the latter is allowed to break in and interrupt the straightforward monster combat, with its troublesome speculation about Heatho-Bard treachery. In other words, the Grendel affair has resolved nothing but itself; it is as self-contained and set apart as the legendary lay it is already turning into. History and men will undo *sib* [kinship] at Heorot more drastically than Grendel ever could.

This prepares us for the final episode, in which the historical "digressions" interrupt the monster fight, indeed crowd it off the page altogether, to claim equal space. The confused, desperate, and ferocious clashings of Swedes and Geats are more urgent and apropos than the heroic but futile showdown between the two venerable *æglæcan*, for that is the narrative which will take over at the end and undo the timeless mythic closure that the extinction of monsters and heroes might imply. Arguments about the state of Beowulf's soul or whether he displays a tragic flaw in his last fight are not really to the point—he is old and must meet his end day, and the circumstances of the dragon fight merely underscore what is bound to happen, the point being that Beowulf's brisk heroism has frozen into a magnificent but nonetheless sterile monumentality: he has no heir, nor is there anyone else strong enough to sustain his holding action upon the disintegrating forces of history. The lonely superman is as much a dinosaur as is his opponent. As the "digressions" culminate in the poem's only narration of a full-scale battle which echoes the paradigmatic monster fights in a thoroughly messy and scrambled fashion, the two narrative modes have collapsed into each other, from a relationship of would-be dialectic to one of mutual deconstruction. As Beowulf and the dragon destroy one another ("hæfde æghwæðer ende gefered / lænan lifes [each of the two had fared to the end of transitory life]" [2844–45]), so—in consequence—will men. Far from resolving the tensions of history, the dragon fight brings them forward, clears a space for them to write themselves out. The poem ends with a stark unresolved chasm between its narrative modes: the monster fight turns out to be a series of epitaphs, legends of fallen grandeur, and all that remains is foreboding of the self-deconstructing enactment of the dynastic codes of feud and vengeance, bitter murder-bale of clans.

Hence the considerable power, both ironic and elegiac, of the poem's end. If the contest of narratives has a theme, it is the failure of the mythic and imaginary mode to resolve or contain what turns out to be privileged as the mode of historical reality. To reify, externalize, mythologize our own tendencies as heroes and monsters, cancelling each other in a metaphysical arena outside time and history, is to seek refuge in a symbolic solution which here does not refuse the grim and poignant knowledge that time and history will resume, that time and history are always present to inscribe the mythic agon with the recognition of its own impossibility. It is the sophisticated representation of this insight that makes the stance of the *Beowulf* poem, for all its historical strangeness, so modern. There is nothing crude or primitive about this complex narrative mediation of the mythical and the historical imaginations.

II

I wish to meditate further on the genre of epitaph with which the poem closes. To get at the force and meaning this might carry, let us return to where we began, Grendel and his analogues. The modernism of the *Beowulf* poet's stance becomes apparent when we consider his monsters alongside those of the Scandinavian sagas, even granted that the latter were in most cases written down centuries afterwards. In the sagas, as the folktales, it is notable that the monsters are both more supernatural and at the same time more natural than they are in *Beowulf*. Magical impossibilities abound, but the text accommodates them with hardly the flicker of a rhetorical eyebrow, suggesting that this is nothing out of the ordinary, that human, natural, and supernatural elements share an unruffled continuum. Here, the monsters are on the one hand "rationalized"—there are no miracles in *Beowulf*, the text adheres to an Aristotelean ethos of probable impossibilities—and yet they are felt to be unknown, mysterious, and Other, *ellorgæstas*, ambassadors from an alien and obscure dimension. They are true denizens of the twilight zone, and the *Beowulf* poet is, as Northrop Frye wittily suggests, the first "Gothic revivalist" in English literature. The poem's stance of lateness and literariness (*in geardagum* [in days of yore]) is expressed in its self-conscious conferral of an epistemologically doubtful status upon its monsters: as Tolkien observes, Grendel is both a cannibalistic wretch, exceptionally powerful and malicious, and a demoniacal shadow-glider. We have said that Grendel's otherness is socially signified, but on an ontological level he defines the boundaries of the human itself. The anthropoid monster is a constant figure of mythological anxiety about the origins and status of the human, up to our contemporary Bigfoot hallucinations and more dangerous racist fantasies: us and yet not us, in our divinely granted image, and yet chthonic, cannibalistic, language-lacking: dark alternative possibilities of our own identity. St. Augustine authorized a patristic tradition defining the equivocal status of a Grendel: in human shape, the divine figure disfigured, the manlike monster or giant therefore is a rational soul bearer and consequently damned. The Grendels share the passion, misery, kinship feeling of men; Hrothgar's *earfoðþrag* [time of tribulation] is the contagion of Grendel's own. They situate, then, the limits of the social as the limits of the human. The homeless home of the monsters is conceived (in Hrothgar's vivid speech) as a generic Gothic outdoors, an anthology of wilderness topoi. It cannot be mapped because (although "Nis þæt feor heonon / milgemearces [it is not far hence by measure of miles]" [1361]) it occupies a dimension outside the human rational and familiar world whose presiding deity is Metod, the Measurer of things visible and invisible. The Grendelfolk are truly *unheimliche* in the Freudian sense: the unhomely ones that define what is homely, also the uncanny ones who define what is familiar or known.

Hence the thematic resonance of one of the first epithets applied to Grendel, along with his name and territory:

> wæs se grimma gæst   Grendel haten,
> mære mearcstapa,   se þe moras heold,
> fen ond fæsten

[the grim spirit was called Grendel, / the notorious boundary-stalker, he who held the moors, / the fen and fastnesses].

(102–4)

He is a "notorious boundary-stalker." The rhetoric of Gothic horror applied to the monsters gains its power from that mysterious otherness beyond boundaries. Beowulf has heard of Grendel as

> sceaðona ic nat hwylc,
> deogol dædhata   deorcum nihtum
> eaweð þurh egsan   uncuðne nið

[an enemy I know not what, / a hidden persecutor (who) in dark nights / shows in a terrible manner unknown ill will].

(274–76)

The monsters straddle the limits of human knowledge that we shall see as thematic throughout the poem:

men ne cunnon,
hwyder helrunan   hwyrftum scriþað.

[men do not know, / whither hell-demons turn their footsteps.]

(162–63)

In fact, most of the "evil" or adversary terms throughout the poem turn out to be associated with mystery or secrecy, with *helrunan* that turn beyond the ken of the human community. Just as Hrothgar's description of the *micle mearcstapan* [great boundary-stalkers] and their *dygel lond* [secret land] is a tissue of reports and conjectures on the known and the not-known, so the dragon occupies a *dryhtsele dyrnne* [mysterious great hall]. Both the dragon's barrow and the Grendelmere are sinister because they are hidden, unknown places, reached with difficulty via steep and narrow paths ("steap stanhlið, stige nearwe, / enge anpaðas, uncuð gelad [the steep rocky slopes, the narrow path, narrow lonely ways, the unknown track]" [1409–10]). Heorot, in contrast, is famous and widely seen, "Sele hlifade / heah ond horngeap [the hall towered high and horn-gabled] (81–82), and easy of access to all:

Stræt wæs stanfah,   stig wisode
gumum ætgædere.

[The street was stone-paved, the path showed the way / to the men together.]

(320–21)

It is instructive in this light to compare the entries of the outsiders, Grendel and Beowulf, into Heorot. While Grendel is a *mearcstapa* whose raid is a horrible violation of boundaries (between inside and outside, hearth and wilderness, culture and cannibal barbarity, human and inhuman, familiar and unknown), Beowulf's approach to Heorot is figured as the proper and right negotiation of a series of frontiers and thresholds. This is the governing trope for that complex and delicate progress of social codifications of which I spoke earlier. Beowulf guides his men to the Geatish *landgemyrcu* [shore], and presently they come to the Danish boundary and the important encounter with its *endesæta*, the Coastguard. The Coastguard is favourably impressed with the *cuðlic* [open] manner of their disembarking, and the rite of crossing is negotiated by a making known of *frumcyn* [lineage, origin] and intent ("ne sceal þær dyrne sum / wesan [nor shall there be anything mysterious]" [271]). In exchange, the

Coastguard will also *cyðan,* make the way known to the visitors. This formal, ritualistic crossing of thresholds proceeds as the Geats arrive at Heorot, encounter Wulfgar, and finally petition Hrothgar himself: the flyting too is a generic variant of this series. This important passage of the poem shows us the social code working as a decorous intersection and negotiation of boundaries by rites of showing and making known which redefine those boundaries: thus the codification of territories, hierarchies, and identities reinscribes itself.

The poem suggests an important homology between the circulation and exchange of treasure, on which the *comitatus* system depends, and this circulation and exchange of words/knowledge, by the trope *wordhord* [or *breosthord*] *onleac* [unlock] (259). The Coastguard's tag thus earns its sententious weight:

> Æghwæþres sceal
> scearp scyldwiga   gescad witan,
> worda ond worca,   se þe wel þenceð.

[Every sharp / shield-warrior must be the judge, / of words and works, he who thinks carefully.]

(287–89)

The excellence of a Beowulf is that he is able to join *wordas* and *worcas* in transparent, performative unity, by carrying out his boasts. When we are told that Unferth *onband beadurune* [let loose battle-runes] (501), the suggestion of hostility and secrecy, "battle-rune," should warn us that this is not the same kind of magnanimous word exchange. For to speak freely and forthrightly is equivalent to the liberal dispensing of rings. The dragon's hoard takes its place in this tropological system: it is sinister because its stagnant, sepulchral occlusion from proper social exchange and circulation is identified with this rhetoric of secrecy. Secrecy in itself generates malignity, breeds dragons:

> Þa wæs gesyne,   þæt se sið ne ðah
> þam ðe unrihte   inne gehydde
> wræte (ms. *wræce*) under wealle.

[Then it was seen, that the venture did not profit / him who unrightly hid inside / the ornaments under the wall.]

(3058–60)

The correlative to this in the human-historical narrative is Heremod, the type of the bad king, who represents the solitary turning away from the community, the treacherous slaughter of kinsmen, and the refusal to dispense treasure. As the moral is pointed later:

                                    he him est geteah
        meara ond maðma.—   Swa sceal mæg don,
        nealles inwitnet   oðrum bregdon
        dyrnum cræfte,   deað ren(ian)
        hondgesteallan.

[he (Hrothgar) gave him the gift, / mares and treasures. So must men do, / not at all weave malice-nets for each other / with secret skill, prepare death / for hand-companions.]

                                                            (2165–69)

Hrothgar's sermon, springing from the Heremod exemplum, exhorts Beowulf to be vigilant against *ignorance*. Vulnerability to secret murder-bale is equated with the determination of a wider horizon of knowing/unknowing:

                                    nallas on gylp seleð
        fætte beagas,   ond he þa forðgesceaft
        forgyteð ond forgymeð,   þæs þe him ær God sealde

        . . . .

        Bebeorh þe ðone bealoni ð,   Beowulf leofa,
        secg betsta,   ond þe þæt selre geceos
        ece rædas

[he, not at all honorable, does not give / ornamental rings, and he his future state forgets and neglects, because of what God gave him before. . . . / Protect yourself against that wickedness, beloved Beowulf, / best man, and choose you the better— / eternal gain].

                                            (1749–51; 1758–60)

The themes of hoard dispensing, secret hate-contrivance, and the metaphysical horizon of knowledge of one's destiny all converge at the end of this important passage. The narrative of the whole poem is in fact motivated by the intersection of perspectives and horizons of knowledge. Brodeur and Renoir have written influential accounts of the celebrated passage in which Grendel stalks Heorot, in terms of a rhetoric of suspense and point of view. The narrative is more precisely articulated, however, by a constant shifting between horizons of perception, intention, anticipation, ignorance, and discovery, and by the degree of their eventual fulfilment and reversal, and by an ultimate perspective, available only as time unfolds, called God or Wyrd.

This rhetoric I have been tracing defines the poem's level of metaphysical commentary and speculation. Questions of whether the poem exhibits a pagan or Christian world view, the relationship between God and Wyrd as authoritative metaphysical terms, have generated much critical contention. The point seems to be, though, that the poem refrains from a final settlement of these issues: such terms are situational and plot variable horizons of the known and not-known within its world. The stance, as toward so much in the poem, is set forth in the opening narrative of Scyld Scefing's obsequies:

> Men ne cunnon
> secgan to soðe,   selerædende,
> hæleð under heofenum,   hwa þæm hlæste onfeng.

[Men do not know / cannot say in truth, (neither) counselors in the hall, / (nor) heroes under heaven, who received that freight.]

(50–52)

The refrain recurs throughout this early part of the poem. The pagan/ Christian stance shifts with deliberate ambiguity, and seems to allow the poet a free space of uncertainty in which he can work.

If God is that always-beyond-our-ken in which we must trust to provide for us, *wyrd* is the negative term for that horizon of knowledge, as that which limits and denies the reach of our will and intellect. As we saw, this becomes increasingly the mode of the latter part of the poem: as social mediations of knowledge, of the definition of boundaries, dissolve away, no one's will or intention can coincide anymore with the turn of the narrative. Gone is the epistemologically sure genre of Beowulf's *gilp-spræc* [boasting speech], a performative utterance which forecasts (thus authors) the issue of the narrative.

I have suggested that the mode of secrecy is connected with the word- and ring-hoarding and *searoniðas* of a Heremod, of the *inwitnet,* feud and kinsman slaughter which generate the etiological narrative of history itself, characterized by *edwenden* that confound any foreknowledge, expectation or stable closure (= peace settlement). History determines us because it is, indeed, a secret runic narrative we cannot read, let alone write, but only try to decipher and chronicle after the fact: wyrd is that which writes us.

The monster-fight narrative, on the other hand, sets itself up as a definitive, once-and-for-all teleology of making-known. That in or among ourselves which we do not know, which is both us and not us, the limits or contradictions of our modes of life which can undo us, we make other, outside—represent in a figure or mythical form which can then be contained, proscribed and annihilated in a symbolic combat. The linear, transparent narrative achieves full closure and final resolution with this abolition of the Uncanny Other; the whole world is rewritten as known, familiar, kith and kin, one universal *sibbegedriht*. Thus the monster fight often concludes with a trope of enlightenment: *beorht beacen Godes* [God's bright beacon] from the East, a glow inside the hate hall like *rodores candel* [heaven's candle] (570; 1572). Unknown ways and places are mapped out on the victorious return: Beowulf and his band march back from the Grendelmere on a *cuþe stræte* [familiar street], the homecoming to Geatland is signalled by the sight of *cuþe naessas* [familiar headlands]. Beowulf becomes the first detective in English literature when he exhorts Hrothgar to go with him to clear up the murder mystery by examining the clues:

> Aris, rices weard,   uton hraþe feran,
> Grendles magan   gang sceawigan.
> Ic hit þe gehate: no he on helm losaþ,
> ne on foldan fæþm,   ne on fyrgenholt,
> ne on gyfenes grund,   ga þær he wille!

[Arise, guardian of the kingdom, let us quickly fare out, / to behold the track of Grendel's kin. / I promise to you: she will not escape under cover, / nor in the earth's bosom, nor in mountain wood, / nor in sea's bottom, go where she will!]

(1390–94)

Gothic horror and mystery give way to something like a scientific discourse of examination and measurement. Gone is a rhetoric of shadow creepers, night fliers, eyes flaming in darkness: we receive a daylight anatomy of Grendel's claw (now a *cuþe folme* [familiar hand] [1303]), and learn that the dead dragon "wæs fiftiges fotgemearces / lang on legere [was fifty footmarks long in the place of his lying]" (3042–43).

It seems very important throughout this poem, in fact, that the monster conflict resolve in something that can be shown to men, a clear sign, a token or trophy. Great narrative weight is put on the fact that Grendel leaves his arm as a "tacen sweotol [clear token]" of his defeat, and his mother's retrieval of it is made to seem almost as catastrophic as her murder of Æschere. This is connected with an important narrative figure pervasive throughout the poem which, for want of a better description, I am going to call its wonder-gazing topos, *wunder-sceawian*. Grendel has left his arm to be nailed up under the gables, and bloody traces on his path:

> ferdon folctogan feorran ond nean
> geond widwegas wundor sceawian,
> laþes lastas.

[folk leaders fared from far and near / from far-extending regions to behold the wonder, / the trace of the hated one.]

(839–41)

Beowulf's first demystifying (scientific) action upon arrival at the occult Grendelmere is to shoot a *wundorlic wægbora* [strange wave-roamer] and have it hauled up on shore: "weras sceawedon / gryrelicne gist [the men examined the horrible visitor]" (1440–41). Beowulf is careful to bring back trophies from the Grendelmere, after the Scyldings have misinterpreted the ambiguous sign of blood on the water. He insists that before he dies Wiglaf show him the dragon hoard ("hord is gesceawod, grimme gegongen [the hoard is examined, grimly attained]" [3084–85]. This has nothing whatever to do with any kind of avarice, as some critics have argued (that belongs to an ethical system quite absent from the poem). Rather, it signifies within the rhetorical system I am describing: the issue is that of a secret or mystery being made known, being discovered to the eyes of men, as a clear sign. The dragon's gold has been malignant because it has been hidden away. The last, futile rallying of the Geatish comitatus after the disaster is in ritual fulfilment of the topos:

> Uton nu efstan oðre [siðe],
> seon ond secean searo[gimma] geþræc,
> wunder under wealle, ic eow wisige,
> þæt ge genoge neon sceawiað
> beagas ond brad gold.

[Let us now hasten another time, / to seek and see the heap of precious jewels, / the wonder under the wall; I shall direct you, / that you behold enough from close up / of rings and broad gold.]

(3101–5)

Both dead monster and dead hero are added to this catalog of wonders to behold:

> Weorod eall aras,
> eodon unbliðe   under Earnanæs,
> wollenteare   wundur sceawian.

[The band all arose, / went unhappily under Earnaness / with welling tears, to look on the wonder.]

(3030–32)

After the battle, the community gathers to reconfirm itself in the collective action of gazing upon the "wonder," the defeated Other. The unknown monster is reduced to a curiosity, a freak-show corpse. That which is now completely known is so because it is dead, definitely past, torn out of history, emptied of further possibilities, to be stuffed with the already written.

Such is the drastic closure which the mythologizing narrative of the monster fight seeks to achieve, a closure which irresistibly claims hero as well as monster. In other words, the inevitable tendency of such a narrative is toward, for the monster, museum or trophy hall with measurements affixed, and for the hero, also overwhelmed by the self-cancelling strategies of the genre that would petrify its lonely *æglæcan* against the dissolving reversals of history: monumentality, the genre of epitaph.

Closely associated with the gathering around to gaze upon the wonder is the gathering around to listen to a wonder, the recitals of the scop which memorialize history out of time. Thus, the exhibition of Grendel's hand is but the centerpiece of a veritable national arts festival, which features a king's thane who undertakes

> sið Beowulfes   snyttrum styrian,
> ond on sped wrecan   spel gerade,
> wordum wrixlan

[Beowulf's venture skillfully to recite, / and successfully to tell an apt story, / with varying words].

(872–74)

The fact that the topical tale of a live Beowulf closes into the monumental tale of a dead hero should warn us:

> Sigemunde gesprong
> æfter deaðdæge   dom unlytel,

> syþðan wiges heard   wyrm acwealde,
> hordes hyrde

[For Sigmund (there) sprang up / after his deathday not little glory / after the war-hard one had killed the worm, / the guardian of the hoard].

(884–87)

The heroic tale inevitably resolves in an epitaph. The *Beowulf* poem concludes, after a full rhetorical dress rehearsal of that inevitability, with Beowulf himself becoming a monument, a beacon to guide seafarers to their *cuþe naessas,* and with his survivors (beginning with Wiglaf) composing his epitaphs, which occupy the final lines of the poem:

> cwædon þæt he wære   wyruldcyning(a)
> manna mildust   ond mon(ðw)ærust,
> leodum liðost   ond lofgeornost.

[they said that he was of world-kings the mildest of men and the gentlest, kindest to his people, and most eager for fame (trans. Donaldson).]

(3180–82)

Fame: the record of the finally-written, the wonder to behold, the out of time, the dead. Just as the genealogy of Scyld, asserting an exuberant (as we look back, always and already self-deconstructing) synthesis of mythology and history, provides a generic signal for the early part of the poem, so the keynote for the last chapter is established with the so-called Lay of the Last Survivor. The poem itself turns into a lay of last survivors, an epitaph for *æglæcan*. Beowulf himself enacts for us our characteristic stance in reading this part of the poem. Realizing that he is going to die:

>   Ða se æðeling giong,
> þæt he bi wealle   wishycgende
> gesæt on sesse;   seah on enta geweorc,
> hu ða stanbogan   stapulum fæste
> ece eorðreced   innan healde.

[Then the nobleman went, / so that by the wall, wise in thought, / he might sit on the seat; he looked at the work of giants, / how the stone arch, fast with pillars, / the eternal earth house held within.]

(2715–19)

It is a powerful moment. The mythic contest has ended not in the world made kin, but in a final mortal loneliness. Beowulf's knowledge of his death accompanies his own wonder gazing, linked now with another Old English poetic topos, the *eald enta geweorc*: the eternal ruins of a great civilization that has passed away serve as a memento mori to the fleeting present (cf. *Wanderer, The Ruin*). The monuments remain, but their transcendence signifies our own transitoriness, that old age shall this generation waste also. As *Beowulf* progresses, the monumental records of past origins grow ambiguous and dark, from the bright mythic-heroic genealogies and creation songs of the opening, through the annals of ancient strife carved on the golden hilt from the Grendel hall, to the dragon hoard itself, a mysterious and sinister, possibly accursed relic, signifying racial extinctions. But Beowulf seems to recognize, in a moment of contemplation which fixes us with him in our reading of the poem, that his affinity with the dragon has extended to a melancholy kinship with this *enta geweorc*.

All that is left, at the end, is the bleak elegiac antithesis between the epitaph—the record of past fame, a genre which provides a synecdoche for the narrative of mythic teleologies and symbolic resolutions frozen out of time—and the prophetic foreknowledge expressed by the Geatish messenger, in a final ironic coincidence of *wyrda* and *worda* (3030), that the unstable etiological determinisms of the narrative of history, deconstructing and reversing all human intentions and achievements, will close in. With this prospect, the poem seems to define itself, too, as *eald enta geweorc*. It is all too appropriate that the epitaphic *Beowulf* should itself have turned out to be a literary last survivor, a monster that resists our taxonomies, a wonder to behold.

Chronology

ca. 410 C.E.	Roman rule in Britain ends.
ca. 500	Germanic peoples (Angles, Saxons, Jutes, etc.) established in much of eastern and southeastern England; Ambrosius Aurelianus and the Britons defeat the Saxons at Mount Baden.
550	Gildas's *On the Fall of Britain*.
ca. 560–616	King Aethelbert (the first English ruler to accept Christianity) reigns in Kent.
597	Gregory the Great sends Saint Augustine as the Church's emissary to Christianize Britain.
ca. 625–700	Sutton Hoo ship burial, which may be the grave of Raedwald, King of East Anglia.
ca. 650–800	Probable period of the composition of *Beowulf*.
ca. 657–680	The poet Caedmon's tenure at the monastery at Streoneshealh.
669–90	Tenure of Theodore, Archbishop of Canterbury.
ca. 686	Last pagan dynasty (on the Isle of Wight) comes to an end.
ca. 700–50	Composition of "The Dream of the Rood."
ca. 731	Bede's *Ecclesiastical History* completed.
ca. 735–804	Reign of Alcuin of York.
757–96	Reign of King Offa of Mercia.
ca. 786	Viking raids begin.
865–77	Viking army conquers Northumbria, East Anglia, and most of Mercia.
871–99	King Alfred's reign in Wessex.
878	Danes defeat Wessex forces at Chippenham; Alfred withdraws to the Somerset marshes.
880	Alfred returns.

886	Alfred captures London.
ca. 892	Compilation of the first *Anglo-Saxon Chronicle*.
893–96	Alfred staves off another Viking army.
937	Aethelstan repels the Kings of Strathclyde and Scotland and the Dublin Norse at the Battle of Brunanburh.
959–75	Reign of Edgar, King of all England; era of great ecclesiastical reform.
ca. 975	Compilation of the Exeter Book.
978	Murder of Edward the Martyr.
979–1016	Reign of Aethelred Unraed; era of Archbishop Wulfstan and Abbot Aelfric of Eynsham.
991	Vikings defeat Ealdorman Byrhtnoth's warriors at the Battle of Maldon on the Blackwater in Essex.
ca. 1000	Probable date of the *Beowulf* manuscript (composition may be contemporary with the manuscript).
1016–35	Reign of Cnut the Viking.
1042–66	Reign of Edward the Confessor.
1066	In January, Harold, Earl of Wessex, assumes the throne; killed October 14 at the Battle of Hastings. King William of Normandy (William the Conqueror) assumes the British throne.
1086	William orders the composition of the Domesday Book.

Contributors

HAROLD BLOOM, Sterling Professor of the Humanities at Yale University, is the author of *The Anxiety of Influence, Poetry and Repression,* and many other volumes of literary criticism. His forthcoming study, *Freud: Transference and Authority,* attempts a full-scale reading of all of Freud's major writings. A MacArthur Prize Fellow, he is general editor of five series of literary criticism published by Chelsea House. During 1987–88, he was appointed Charles Eliot Norton Professor of Poetry at Harvard University.

J. R. R. TOLKIEN was Merton Professor of the English Language at Oxford University. A well-known writer of fantasy, he was also one of the century's greatest philologists. He was named a Commander of the British Empire in 1972.

T. A. SHIPPEY is Fellow of St. John's College, Oxford, and the author of *Poems of Wisdom and Learning in Old English.*

ROBERTA FRANK is Professor of English at the University of Toronto. She is coeditor of *A Plan for the Dictionary of Old English* and the author of *Old Norse Court Poetry: The Drattkvaett Stanza.*

RAYMOND P. TRIPP, JR., is Professor of English at the University of Denver. He is the author of many articles on medieval English literature and of *More about the Fight with the Dragon.*

FRED C. ROBINSON is Douglas Tracy Smith Professor of English at Yale University and the author of Beowulf *and the Appositive Style.*

IAN DUNCAN is Assistant Professor of English at Yale University.

Bibliography

Andersson, Theodore M. "Tradition and Design in *Beowulf*." In *Old English Literature in Context,* edited by John D. Niles, 90–206. Bury St. Edmonds, England: Brewer-Rowan & Littlefield, 1980.

Batchelor, C. C. "The Style of *The Beowulf*." *Speculum* 12 (1937): 330–42.

Bessinger, Jess B., Jr., and Stanley J. Kahrl, eds. *Essential Articles for the Study of Old English Poetry.* Hamden, Conn.: Archon, 1968.

Bloomfield, Morton W. "Patristics and Old English Literature: Notes on Some Poems." *Comparative Literature* 14 (1962): 36–43.

———, ed. *The Interpretation of Narrative.* Cambridge: Harvard University Press, 1970.

Bolton, W. F. *Alcuin and Beowulf.* New Brunswick, N.J.: Rutgers University Press, 1978.

Bonjour, Adrian. *The Digressions in Beowulf.* Medium Ævum Monographs, Vol. 5. Oxford: Basil Blackwell, 1950.

———. *Twelve Beowulf Papers, 1940–1960.* Geneva: Librairie E. Droz, 1962.

Brodeur, Arthur. *The Art of Beowulf.* Berkeley: University of California Press, 1960.

Brown, Alan. "The Firedrake in *Beowulf*." *Neophilologus* 64 (1980): 439–60.

Carrigan, Eamon. "Structure and Thematic Development in *Beowulf*." *Proceedings of the Royal Irish Academy* 66, C, 1 (1967): 1–51.

Chadwick, H. Munro. *The Heroic Age.* Cambridge: Cambridge University Press, 1912.

Chambers, R. W. *Beowulf: An Introduction.* Cambridge: Cambridge University Press, 1967.

Cherniss, Michael D. *Ingeld and Christ: Heroic Concepts and Values in Old English Poetry.* The Hague: Mouton, 1972.

Creed, Robert P. *Old English Poetry: Fifteen Essays.* Providence, R.I.: Brown University Press, 1967.

Domico, Helen. *Beowulf's Wealtheow and the Valkyrie Tradition.* Madison: University of Wisconsin Press, 1984.

Donohue, Charles. "*Beowulf* and Christian Tradition: A Reconsideration from a Celtic Stance." *Traditio* 21 (1965): 55–116.

———. "*Beowulf,* Ireland, and the Natural Good." *Traditio* 7 (1949–51): 262–77.

Engelhardt, George J. "*Beowulf* 3150." *MLN* 68 (1953): 535–38.

———. "*Beowulf:* A Study in Dilation." *PMLA* 70 (1955): 825–52.

135

Gardner, Thomas. "The Old English Kenning: A Characteristic Feature of Germanic Poetical Diction?" *Modern Philology* 67 (1969): 109–17.

Goldsmith, Margaret E. "The Christian Perspective in *Beowulf.*" In *Studies in Old English in Honor of Arthur G. Brodeur,* edited by Stanley B. Greenfield, 71–90. Eugene: University of Oregon Books, 1963.

———. *The Mode and Meaning of* Beowulf. London: Athlone, 1970.

Greenfield, Stanley B. *A Critical History of Old English Literature.* New York: New York University Press, 1965.

———. "The Authenticating Voice in *Beowulf.*" *Anglo-Saxon England* 5 (1976): 51–62.

Helterman, Jeffrey. "*Beowulf:* The Archetype Enters History." *ELH* 35 (1968): 1–20.

Huppé, Bernard F. *The Hero in the Earthly City: A Reading of* Beowulf. Binghamton: State University of New York at Binghamton, 1984.

Irving, Edward B., Jr. *Introduction to* Beowulf. Englewood Cliffs, N.J.: Prentice-Hall, 1969.

———. *A Reading of* Beowulf. New Haven: Yale University Press, 1968.

Jones, Gwyn. *Kings, Beasts, and Heroes.* London: Oxford University Press, 1972.

Ker, W. P. *The Dark Ages.* Edinburgh and London: William Blackwood & Sons, 1923.

———. *Epic and Romance: Essays on Medieval Literature.* 2d ed. London: Macmillan, 1908.

Kiernan, Kevin S. Beowulf *and the* Beowulf *Manuscript.* New Brunswick, N.J.: Rutgers University Press, 1981.

Lawrence, William. Beowulf *and the Epic Tradition.* New York: Hafner, 1961.

Lee, Alvin. *The Guest Hall of Eden.* New Haven: Yale University Press, 1972.

Leyerle, John. "The Interlace Structure of *Beowulf.*" *University of Toronto Quarterly* 37 (1967–68): 1–17.

Lord, Alfred B. *The Singer of Tales.* Cambridge: Harvard University Press, 1960.

McGalliard, John C. "The Poet's Comment in *Beowulf.*" *Studies in Philology* 75 (1978): 243–70.

McTurk, R. W. "Variation in *Beowulf* and the *Poetic Edda.*" In *The Dating of* Beowulf, edited by Colin Chase, 141–60. Toronto: The Centre for Medieval Studies and the University of Toronto Press, 1981.

Mitchell, Bruce. "'Until the Dragon Comes . . . ': Some Thoughts on *Beowulf.*" *Neophilologus* 47 (1963): 126–38.

Nicholson, Lewis E., ed. *An Anthology of* Beowulf *Criticism.* Notre Dame, Ind.: University of Notre Dame Press, 1963.

Nicholson, Lewis E., and Dolores Frese, eds. *Anglo-Saxon Poetry: Essays in Appreciation for John C. McGalliard.* Notre Dame, Ind.: Notre Dame University Press, 1975.

Niles, John D. Beowulf: *The Poem and Its Tradition.* Cambridge: Harvard University Press, 1983.

Ogilvy, J. D. A., and Donald Baker. *Reading* Beowulf: *An Introduction to the Poem, Its Background, and Its Style.* Norman: University of Oklahoma Press, 1984.

Opland, Jeff. *Anglo-Saxon Oral Poetry: A Study of the Traditions.* New Haven: Yale University Press, 1980.

Pope, John C. "Beowulf's Old Age." In *Philological Essays: Studies in Old and Middle*

English Language and Literature in Honor of Herbert Dean Merritt, edited by James Rosier. The Hague: Mouton, 1970.

Renoir, Alain. *"Beowulf:* A Contextual Introduction." In *Heroic Epic and Saga,* edited by Felix J. Oinas, 99–119. Bloomington: Indiana University Press, 1978.

Robinson, Fred C. Beowulf *and the Appositive Style.* Knoxville: University of Tennessee Press, 1985.

Shippey, T. A. *Old English Verse.* London: Hutchinson University Library, 1972.

Short, Douglas. *"Beowulf* and Modern Critical Tradition." In *A Fair Day in the Affections: Literary Essays in Honor of Robert B. White, Jr.,* edited by Jack D. Durant and M. Thomas Heater, 1–23. Raleigh, N.C.: Winston Press, 1980.

Sisam, Kenneth. *The Structure of* Beowulf. Oxford: Oxford University Press, 1965.

Stevens, Martin. "The Structure of *Beowulf:* From Gold-hoard to Word-hoard." *Modern Language Quarterly* 39 (1978): 219–38.

Stevens, Martin, and Jerome Mandel, eds. *Old English Literature.* Lincoln: University of Nebraska Press, 1968.

Stevick, Robert D. "The Oral-Formulaic Analysis of Old English Verse." *Speculum* 37 (1962): 382–89.

Watts, Ann C. *The Lyre and the Harp: A Comparative Reconsideration of Oral Tradition in Homer and Old English Epic Poetry.* New Haven: Yale University Press, 1969.

Weil, Simone. *The* Iliad, *or the Poem of Force.* Wallingford, Pa.: Pendle Hill, 1956.

Whallon, William. *Formula, Character, and Context: Studies in Homeric, Old English, and Old Testament Poetry.* Washington, D.C.: The Center for Hellenic Studies, 1969.

Wrenn, Charles L. *A Study of Old English Literature.* London: G. C. Harrap, 1972.

Acknowledgments

"*Beowulf*: The Monsters and the Critics" by J. R. R. Tolkien from *The Monsters and the Critics and Other Essays*, edited by Christopher Tolkien, © 1983 by Frank William Richardson and Christopher Reuel Tolkien as Executors of the Estate of J. R. R. Tolkien. Reprinted by permission of Houghton Mifflin Company and Allen & Unwin Ltd. This essay was first published in *The Proceedings of the British Academy* 22 (1936). Reprinted by permission.

"The World of the Poem" by T. A. Shippey from *Beowulf* by T. A. Shippey, © 1978 by T. A. Shippey. Reprinted by permission of the author and Edward Arnold (Publishers) Ltd.

"The *Beowulf* Poet's Sense of History" by Roberta Frank from *The Wisdom of Poetry: Essays in Early English Literature in Honor of Morton W. Bloomfield,* edited by Larry D. Benson and Siegfried Wenzel, © 1982 by the Board of Trustees of the Medieval Institute. Reprinted by permission of Medieval Institute Publications, Western Michigan University, Kalamazoo, Michigan.

"Digressive Revaluations" by Raymond P. Tripp, Jr. from *More About the Fight with the Dragon:* Beowulf 2208b–3182, Commentary, Edition, and Translation, © 1983 by University Press of America. Reprinted by permission of the University Press of America.

"Apposed Word Meanings and Religious Perspectives" by Fred C. Robinson from Beowulf *and the Appositive Style* by Fred C. Robinson, © 1985 by the University of Tennessee Press. Reprinted by permission of the University of Tennessee Press.

"Epitaphs for Æglæcan: Narrative Style in *Beowulf*" by Ian Duncan, © 1987 by Ian Duncan. Published for the first time in this volume. Printed by permission. Translations supplied by the editor.

Index

Aelfric, 96, 101, 107
Aeneid (Virgil), *Beowulf* compared to, 4, 22, 25, 60, 85, 88
Aeschere, 46–47
Alain de Lille, 54
Alcuin, 54, 55, 56
Alcuin and Beowulf (Bolton), 55
Aldhelm (bishop of Sherborne), 54, 55, 99
Alfred (king of Wessex), 56, 58, 61, 84
Andersson, Theodore M., 68
Andreas (anonymous), 13, 70
Anglo-Saxon Chronicles (anonymous), 89
Arator, 99, 100
Augustine, Saint, 121
Azarias (anonymous), 95

Bately, Janet, 90
Battle of Brunanburh (anonymous), 59
Battle of Maldon, The (anonymous), 16, 59
Bede, the Venerable, 54, 55, 57, 95
Beowulf (anonymous): *Aeneid* compared to, 4, 22, 25, 60, 85, 88; apposition in, 2, 3, 4, 82–87, 88–90, 91–92, 93–95, 96–97, 98–101, 102–7, 108, 109; background of, 1; balance and harmony in, 26, 27; Christian elements in, 1–3, 4, 17–18, 20, 24–25, 47, 57–58, 59, 69, 81–82, 84–86, 87, 88–89, 91–92, 93, 94–95, 97–99, 100–101, 102–3, 104–7, 109, 125; *Consolation of Philosophy* compared to, 56; courage as theme in, 2, 19, 21; criticism re-

garding, 5–16, 17–19, 20, 25, 26, 28, 29, 34, 55, 63–64, 66, 67–68, 69, 73, 81, 87, 88, 98–99, 104, 105, 111, 117, 120, 124, 127; cultural diversity in, 52–53, 54, 55; death as theme in, 21, 24, 30; digressions in, 10–11, 14, 15, 25, 26, 28, 63–69, 70–72, 73–77, 78–79, 112, 117, 119; dynastic elements in, 53, 54, 117–18; emotions as depicted in, 36–39; as epic, 28, 68; epitaphs in, 120, 129–30; ethics and morality in, 39, 58, 73; etiquette in, 36, 49; fate as theme in, 4, 98–99, 100–101, 121; Finnsburh episode in, 44, 71; folktales, legends, and myths in, 9, 12, 14, 17, 18, 19–20, 24, 25, 26, 28, 30, 49, 53, 60, 65, 71, 84; gift giving in, 40, 71, 123–24, 125; glory, honor, and praise in, 2, 4, 25, 40–41, 42–43; good vs. evil in, 112, 122; *Gylfaginning* compared to, 20; *Hamðismál* compared to, 98; hate-contrivance in, 123–24; heroic elements in, 2, 4, 16, 20, 24, 28–29, 36, 49, 58, 59, 61, 109; as historical document, 6–7, 15, 18–19, 20, 24, 25, 30, 49, 51–55, 57, 60–61, 82, 109, 117–18, 119; Icelandic sagas compared to, 10, 19, 22–23, 84, 86, 87, 102, 103; ignorance vs. knowledge in, 124–26; importance of halls in, 44–46; importance of weapons in, 40, 41–42, 43–44; interaction of narrative genres in,